The Tao of Rowdy

Also by Meadow DeVor

Money Love:
A Guide to Changing the Way You Think About Money

The Tao of Rowdy

by

Meadow DeVor

and

The Rowdies

2013

www.MeadowDeVor.com

ISBN-13: 978-1483934587

ISBN-10: 1483934586

Printed in the United States of America

First Printing 2013

for the
Rowdy
in you

CONTENTS

-Preface-

What I really want you to know about me is that I feel the same feelings that you do. I have felt despair and I know how deep it cuts. Crushing loneliness. White hot fury. The deflated sense of helplessness. I have felt defeat.

I have also felt passion that could light up the sky. And laughter that makes me want to burst. And sweet triumph from taking a risk, knowing the win was mine. And compassion so thick that it binds me to another soul. And love that feels so strong I wonder if it will break me.

You and I... we connect at these places. The places where we have hurt and healed. If we show each other the wounds, the scars, the healing, you'll know that this is the only conversation worth having.

If you really knew me, you'd know that I am a tough, direct, go-getter. You'd know that I'm not afraid of asking, or answering, difficult questions. You'd know that I love the truth. And that I still continue to stretch the depths of my authenticity. And that this practice is difficult for me.

You'd know that I love my work, and the women that I get to work with, as much as my own heartbeat.

You'd know that I am crazy, and insecure, and that I'm not really polite. You'd know that sometimes I'm afraid to show up. To tell you who I am. To risk not being liked. And to brave being rejected.

If you really knew me, you'd see. We are more alike than different. We are built of the same stuff. We both suffer when we believe painful stories. And we both experience the same freedom when we give permission to reality.

Loving ourselves is a work in progress. It takes practice. And compassion. It takes commitment. And patience.

If you really knew me, you'd know, that ultimately, it's not so much about whether or not you like me.

It's about whether or not I showed up.

Enough.

For you to have an opinion.

Meadow DeVor

San Luis Obispo, CA

March 2013

-Acknowledgments-

Kira. I know you're going to roll your eyes and try to shush this away so sit down and please just listen for a second. This. *The Rowdies*. The community. The classes. The work we do. This book. You, First Follower, made this possible. Without you, I'd just be a Lone Nut. You turned me into a leader. Thank you.

Lizzie. You know what you said. When and why you said it. And how much I needed to hear it. Thank you.

Tara. You make me want to be a better teacher, coach and human being. You teach me strength and you brought me back to God. For which, I am eternally grateful. Thank you.

Brooke. For Santa Monica and grocery stores. You speak it. Thank you.

Tina. For helping me with this project. For your brilliant writing classes. For the many hours you spent helping me write and edit. For all of your attention and care to help each Rowdy contribute a polished piece of art. For helping us create this beautiful book. Thank you.

Superstar, Smith, Bettina, P, Susan and Susan, Jen, Tara, Tina, Wendy, Ivonne, Kira, Pat, Kristen, 2-L, Kath, Aud, Em, Martine, Cindy, Janelle, Jami, Darla and Marybeth. For spilling your hearts out on paper. For your vulnerability. For your Rowdiness. For telling us your story. Thank you.

Rowdies. My soul sisters. My teachers. My coaches. My students. My friends. Your work makes this world a better place. I am so grateful to have you in my life. And so honored that you've allowed me to be in yours. Thank you.

-Introduction-

Dropping Keys

The small man
builds cages for everyone
he knows.
While the sage,
who has to duck his head
when the moon is low,
keeps dropping keys all night long
for the
beautiful
Rowdy
prisoners.

-Hafiz

My name is Meadow DeVor. I'm a mother, daughter, friend, student, author, teacher, life coach, and a Rowdy. I teach tools and strategies for how to live inspiring, meaningful and happier lives to women from all over the world.

Years ago I co-taught a class where we would use poetry as a tool for inspiration and self-growth. One of the student favorites was "Dropping Keys" by Hafiz, a 14th century Persian poet.

I love this poem. I love the image of the sage who is so big he has to duck his head under the moon. I love the idea of the small man who builds cages.

We all do this. We build cages and believe in them so much that we forget that we hold the key that sets us free. We forget that we are all Beautiful *Rowdy Prisoners*. That we are beautiful in our uniqueness, in our intent to learn, to stretch, to love and to forgive. We are Rowdy because none of us want to be stuck behind those bars. We clang our fists against them and fight with the imaginary cages that hold us back.

We take turns being the sage for each other. We duck our heads under the moon and drop keys for each other. The keys to free us from the prison that we have built for ourselves. The cage that the smaller part of us built to keep us safe.

I love that the sage isn't giving the *Rowdy prisoners* the keys. He's dropping them. The prisoner still needs to pick that key up and unlock their own cage. This is a brilliant metaphor for self work.

Because of this poem my students began calling themselves the *Rowdy Prisoners*. And this became the core group of women that continued to take my classes. These students continued to further my stretch as a teacher. And forged their journey right to the center of their own lives. These women are now the backbone of a thriving world-wide community devoted to a daily practice of self-growth and self-discovery.

Over time, we've dropped the word 'prisoners' - and now we just call ourselves *The Rowdies.*

I developed the Rowdy Community because I saw that some of my students were making radical changes in their lives. They were able to completely overhaul the way they thought, the way they reacted to turmoil and were dramatically changing tangible results in their lives.

And then some of my students tended to kind of just stay in the same place. They were committed to self-growth and they had the desire to learn but they lacked something.

What they lacked was practice.

My students who were kicking ass were not only just working with me on a weekly basis. They were in my classes. On my forums. Getting online help on a daily basis. They emailed me constantly. They journaled.

They had a daily practice. They weren't just trying to fit in their personal development in between their activities on any-given-Thursday. They made a commitment to do this work every day.

We all need this. We're not going to accidentally land in an outstanding extraordinary life that we imagine for ourselves. We have to learn how to live it. We have to practice the concepts. A lot.

Happiness isn't a destination; it's a skill. And any skill can be learned with practice.

I have found that there is something magical about adding the element of a living, breathing community of women who are all supporting each other. They are all practicing the new concepts that they learn in class each week. They are missed when they haven't shown up. They hold each other, their own self and me to incredibly high standards. We send bitchslaps, high fives and hugs through cyberspace. We cheer for our wins. And cry for our losses.

Most importantly - we are all speaking the same language. The language of stretching ourselves to be what we really came here to be. Extraordinary women. Women who matter.

These women are just like you and me. We are stay-home-moms, business owners, designers, accountants, and lawyers. We are daughters. Mothers. Friends. Teachers and students.

We might volunteer way too often or have trouble saying no. We might be feeling a little guilty or maybe feeling a lot stuck. We are women who might struggle with insecurity - or maybe we just want to lose a little bit of weight. We are women who want to pay off our debt - or are trying to find enough courage to leave our job and start a new career.

We are women who want to love unconditionally - although we still might harbor a bit of resentment. We are women who want to parent flawlessly - but might struggle with the fear of letting our kids go free into this world.

Basically, we are real women, with everyday issues. Looking for a better way to think about our lives.

We are women that want to feel free. In our relationships. In our families. In our finances. And most of all, in our own skin.

We are women that are on the edge of something bigger. We can feel it in our bones.

We know that there's something more out there for us and we are constantly looking for tools and strategies that can help us reach for a life that is evolving. Inspired. Fulfilled.

Tao (pronounced 'dow') is an ancient Chinese word meaning 'way' or 'path.' In this book, you will be given tools in the form of *Rowdyisms* that will start to show you this 'way' of living a Rowdy life. The way of strength. The way of peace. The way of acceptance. The way of courage. The way of love. For yourself. For others. For life itself.

I did not invent these ideas. No one did. The 'way' can't be invented. Or created. Or taken credit for. This wisdom is merely intrinsic in reality. It can only be discovered within your own experience and then taught to others so that they can discover it for themselves. These teachings have been around for thousands of years. I have merely chosen long-established teachings and modernized them. Given them current language. Given this old wisdom a voice for women in today's experience.

For this reason, I've chosen to share these teachings with you. But not solely through my voice and my experience. I want you to experience this through the voice of *the Rowdies* themselves. Through their understanding of these concepts. Through their struggles. And through their truth-seeking.

These women are my students. And they are also my teachers. Sisters. Friends. Colleagues. And the inspiration for my work in this world.

The *Tao of Rowdy* is a collection of ideas and principles that we practice. A code for living. The way you choose to experience this book is up to you. You may simply want to silently ask a question and then open this book up and read whatever happens to be on that page. Or you may want to scan through the *Rowdyisms* and choose something that speaks to you. You may want to read the entire book start to finish. Over and over. Follow your own lead here. If something resonates with you, keep it. And leave everything else. As you continue to study these concepts, you'll start to see a pattern. And you'll start to stretch your mind to incorporate this new way of perceiving the world.

For each Rowdyism, I've included a series of questions ("Rowdy Up") to help you deepen your practice and personalize your understanding of the concept. Your answers to these questions change depending on circumstances and experience. This work isn't something to just check off a list. Or to be done with. I encourage you to return to questions that moved you. Shifted you. Spoke to you.

I encourage you to see this as a practice. As something to incorporate into your life on a daily basis.

These concepts might be difficult to understand. They might make you angry. Or sad. They might bring up all kinds of stuff for you to look at. To question. They might pull that mask that you cling to right off your face. They might leave you feeling naked. Exposed. Vulnerable.

And that's ok.

That's the work that Rowdies do. Because we know that all the good stuff in life happens when those masks are off. When we show up as ourselves. When we fall in love with that raw, vulnerable and beautiful woman that we see reflected in the mirror.

Rowdies don't take life at face value. We know that we are responsible for how we think. For how we feel. For what we do and for the results we get in our lives. We question everything. We tell the truth. We set goals. We reach. Hard.

This work is hard. This work that we do together is not for the namby-pambies. It's not for the people who want to be spoon fed. It's not for the people who want to be saved by a fairy-tale fantasy. Mastering our life seems hard. Because it is.

This work is for bad-ass women who are willing to look their worst fears in the eye and say, "Bring it." This work is for women who are willing to stick it out. Women who are willing to face themselves and their beliefs. Women who are willing to rock their world, dissolve their identity, to give up life as they know it.

Women who are willing to walk out into the unknown and have an adventure. In search for their own peace of mind.

Women who want to change. And are willing to do the hard work. This work is for the leaders. The brave ones. The go-getters. The explorers. The innovators.

The Rowdies.
This work is for women.
Just like you.

Chapter 1

· · · · · · · · · · · · ·

A Rowdy knows that she is responsible for what she thinks, how she feels, what she does and for the results she creates in her life.

Meadow DeVor

Let's get this straight.

I have never been a docile, passive or victim-y person. I have never appeared to be the damsel-in-distress-type. I've always had my snappy comebacks. My audaciously loud laugh. My sassy independence.

Yet for most of my adult life, concealed behind the tough exterior, was a woman (girl) secretly waiting to be saved. I believed that if I just had the right guy. Or the right job. Or the right body. Or the right family. Or maybe if I lived in the right place. Or fell into enough money.

That everything would be ok. That I would finally be safe. Lovable.

That I would feel at home. That I would belong.

I didn't want to admit this. Not to myself. Not to those around me. I've always considered myself independent. A go-getter. A leader. I hid the truth. I was scared. Lonely. And wanting to latch onto anything or anybody that could save me.

The more I wanted to be saved the more I drowned. Choking on my insecurity. My fear. My shame. I clung to people that seemed strong enough for both of us. I gave up my pieces of my life. My voice. Believing that loyalty and loss-of-self were the price I would have to pay for safety. For love.

Absolutely devastated to learn that my self-appointed-saviors had no intention of saving me. Not understanding that even if they wanted to. They couldn't have.

I found myself in the middle of a life that I had single-handedly created.

I had gotten myself deeply into debt. A newly divorced mom of a little girl who desperately needed me to be strong. For her. For us. My career was in crisis. My identity had been uprooted. I didn't know who to be. Who I was. What I believed in. Or who I wanted to become.

I was drowning.

And no amount of money. No man. No friend. No family could save me from myself. From my own insecurities. From my own self-inflicted limitations.

I needed to learn how to swim that sea on my own.

All this thrashing around waiting, wishing and hoping for help was getting me nowhere. No one was coming to save me. And then it clicked.

I could save myself. And I did. And I continue to.

By taking responsibility for my life. By taking responsibility for my feelings. My actions. And for the results that I create. By owning my choices and by speaking with my own voice.

I've learned that there is no greater safety than being willing to lose everything. Again and again. I've learned that the thing we usually run from is the thing we need to walk directly into. Whether it is confrontation, failure or fear. Running from things only makes them worse.

I've learned that there is no greater expression of love than being willing to have our hearts broken. To be willing to share ourselves. Wide open. Is the greatest gift that life has to offer.

I've learned that everything is truly ok. Even when it seems like it's not. And we must trust that given enough time everything makes sense in the end. I've learned that we don't need to find a home. We carry home with us. Instead of waiting to belong to someone. We can spend our lives belong-ing ourselves to others.

I've learned that we all have moments where we wish and hope that someone can swoop in and save us. We all have things that seem like too much to bear. Too much to change. Too much to carry on our own.

But if we lean on someone else, or wait for someone else to save us, we end up weakening ourselves. We become more susceptible to injury. We lose sight of our own power.

Rowdies know that ultimately, we are responsible for our reaction to our minds. We are responsible for what we feel and for what we do in our lives. We are not damsels in distress - we are the heroes of our stories.

We take this privilege seriously.

And we want you to as well.

You're the only one who can get you where you really want to go.

Trust yourself.

You are so much stronger than you think.

ROWDY UP.

Life is constantly handing us new adventures. The universe is up to all sorts of things with and without our consent. People behave the way they behave (whether we like it or not). Weather, friends, family, jobs, money, bodies. These are all neutral circumstances. Part of reality. We don't get to choose what happens - but we do get to choose how we react. How we choose to think about it. How we choose to feel about it. The actions (or lack of action) that we take. And for the ultimate results that we create through our beliefs and behavior.

What results do I want to create in my life?

_____

What actions are required to create those results?

_____

What obstacles might stand in my way?

_____

How can I take responsibility for overcoming those obstacles?

_____

What blame do I need to let go of in order to create the results I want?

_____

Who or what do I need to forgive?

_____

What do I need to believe in order to achieve what I really want?

_____

What do I need to believe about myself in order to do what it takes?

_____

Chapter 2
. . . .

A Rowdy questions everything.

Bettina Ende-Henningsen

Everything? Yes – everything.

I always have seen myself as an inquiring mind. After all, I am a neuroscientist – a person trained to ask questions, to validate data, to search for the source. But what about the things going on in my own life? I never realized that I was taking so many thoughts and beliefs for granted.

Rowdies, however, question everything. They ask each other – is this true? Is this thought serving you? Is this bringing you closer to who you really are? Who would you be if you didn't believe this?

Questioning means wanting to know. It does not mean knowing better. It does not mean imposing any suggestions on one another. Questioning means wanting to clarify, wanting to open doors so that the light can shine in. Most important is the awareness that, by questioning someone else's thoughts, you are always questioning your own thoughts as well.

This takes practice. Sometimes, you might hit on a powerful question that will be followed by a landslide of insight. But more often, it's not about the big question which will turn your world around in a moment. It's more like a continuous flow of questions and answers that call for new questions. It's like the lapping of small waves. They seem soft and gentle, but in the long run they have the power to erode rocks.

One of my own hardest rocks is my relationship to food. I have been struggling with under and overeating, body shape and weight for many years of my life. A diagnosis of "eating disorder" was attached in my teenage years, and it stuck. Most firmly, it stuck in my mind. Most of my life, I told myself the story that I wasn't able to deal with food in a normal way. I told myself the story that food was a threat. I even believed that having to cook for my family was an almost impossible demand for a woman with "my disease."

But one day, the Rowdy question "Who would you be if you stopped labeling yourself as a woman with an eating disorder?" was thrown at me. Without that question, I would never have considered that possibility. As I committed to answer it, my deeply buried soul started to expand and to repossess the whole me, body included. It was a truly transformative process. I started seeing myself as a healthy woman with a neutral weight and body. A woman who started to feel undamaged and unbroken. A woman handling neutral food. A woman standing in her kitchen, washing potatoes, chopping fresh green herbs with a red knife, breading a slice of meat, smelling delicious smells of onions and garlic sizzling in olive oil. No threat about that.

And the questions kept coming. How does this food really

taste? Which feelings am I trying to avoid by eating? What happens if I decide to feel them? What do I choose to see in the mirror? What does the number on the scale mean? Does it mean anything at all? Why does it seem so important?

Will this process ever be finished? Well, as *the Rowdies* would say, "Great question - answer it!"

Tina Sederholm

From an early age I scooped large forkfuls of food into my mouth, barely chewing more than once or twice before swallowing. I learned this from my Dad, whose stepfather insisted that my father and his siblings eat as quickly and silently as possible before leaving the table so he himself could enjoy his meal in peace. Who he learned it from…well, who knows.

I never questioned this behavior, nor the rules at school. There, we were compelled to take a portion of all the food on offer. Teachers and prefects watched us to make sure we cleared our plates. There was plenty of rumor and innuendo about the consequence of not eating everything, and as I was terrified of getting into trouble, I always made sure I was first to finish.

Come adulthood and I wore this behavior as a badge of pride. Eating really fast, or while driving, or in front of my computer, I could get to the next client or task sooner. Chocolate was my particular weakness, and I ate it in handfuls, never leaving a sliver in the wrapper. Then I'd feel the insidious leech of guilt afterwards. I told myself this was just the way I was. Shrugged my shoulders and always kept a packet of Tums in my handbag.

One day I was at a buffet lunch with a group of fellow poets. Several trays of chocolates were laid out for dessert. I had four on the side of my plate and from time to time I glanced over and wondered about how many I could take without appearing greedy.

While plotting my return to the buffet, the man sitting across from me picked up a chocolate. He inspected it closely, turning it this way and that, as if he were a jeweler, holding it up to the light. Then he lifted that chocolate to his mouth, and bit off less than half. His eyes softened as he chewed, the strawberry flavored fondant slipping over his tongue. Then he put the other half down and started talking to the woman next to him. Sweat prickled my armpits. How could he laugh at someone's joke when there was still chocolate waiting to be eaten?

Finally he picked up the other half, but hesitated. Maybe he was considering if the chocolate was too cloying for his tastes. Even I had winced at its chemical aftertaste. Perhaps he was acknowledging it, like a Native American silently thanking the animal he has just slaughtered.

I don't know. But what I do know was that I was hungry for an experience like that. Having a choice. Savoring food. Watching him provoked me to question my own behaviors around eating.

Asking, "Why do I eat until doubled over with indigestion?"
Answering, "I eat when I feel sad, angry or scared. Eating dis-

tracts me from the feeling."

"What would happen if you felt the feeling?"

"I don't know. I'm not used to feeling them."

Feeling my feelings can seem dangerous. A tidal wave threatening to drown me. But when I allow that wave to wash though me, instead of overwhelming me, it floods out. It's intense for a minute or two. Then it's gone. The surge settles, and I can move on. So different to the dull ache of feelings suppurating and solidifying under a hunk of food.

Questioning my thoughts and actions isn't easy. It doesn't always make me feel better. But it has the sense of right action about it. And it tastes of freedom. Like the sweetness of a fresh fig, not the saccharine flavor of cheap strawberry fondant.

ROWDY UP

Questioning creates an innate ability to find peace wherever we land in life. We question the status quo. The socially acceptable. We question what our moms taught us. And what our dad may not have taught us. We question what the banks tell us to do. What the beauty industry tells us to do. We question advice we get from our mentors, our peers and our students. But, most of all, we question our own beliefs. We are constantly searching for what is even more true than we originally thought.

What am I feeling right now?

_____

Why am I feeling this?

_____

What is my mind saying about this?

_____

Is the thought true?

_____

Is the thought useful?

_____

Is the thought kind?

_____

How can I show my mind the way to harmony?

_____

What story is my mind chewing on?

_____

Is my mind's story based in the past or in the future?

_____

Who is the "I" that is speaking in my mind?

_____

Who is the "I" that is responding to to my mind?

_____

Is my mind in my control or is it being compulsive?

_____

Chapter 3

A Rowdy knows that it's impossible for someone to make her feel something without her consent.

Michele Smith

If you wait for someone else to make you feel like you belong or that you are loved, you will never truly belong and you will never really be loved.

I didn't always know this.

Arriving at my CrossFit gym one evening to work out, a group of my friends was leaving to go out to dinner. Someone asked me if I wanted to go but I declined, saying I wanted to get my workout in. While changing in the locker room, I heard a few of my friends going through great effort to convince another person to skip working out to go with them. When I came out of the bathroom, everyone was gone and I felt pissed and rejected.

No one had tried to persuade me to skip working out to go to dinner. No one said good-bye. No one made me feel special. I wanted to drop them as friends so they couldn't leave me out anymore, despite the fact that this group of people had shown me time and again that they did love me. Basically, I was a forty-one year-old woman behaving like a five year-old.

I had forgotten that Rowdies believe that love can't land on you. It comes from the inside out. I can't feel loved without my consent. I can't feel special unless I decide to. Neither can I feel left-out without my own story spinning in my mind.

I used to think that whether or not I belonged in any group or individual friendship depended upon other people and, more importantly, whether they liked me. This meant I was constantly making other people responsible for my feelings. I looked to other people to tell me how to feel about myself. About our relationships. About my worthiness. Or my belonging.

What I've learned now is that I am the only one responsible for my feelings – through my thoughts and by opening up my heart to the greater love accessible to all of us, in myself and in the other. This requires asking what I am giving, rather than looking for what I am not getting.

I needed to learn that other people's opinions of me do not control the way I feel. I, alone, create my own feelings. Through my own beliefs. My mind. My experience.

Sometimes, like that night at the gym, I fall back into old painful stories about needing to be special or loved by others. Putting other people in charge of my feelings of belonging, safety and trust. Recently at a Rowdy Retreat in California, I found these feeling surfacing again - not belonging, not being important to others. This time, I decided the best solution was to run back home to my husband and my kids who I knew loved me. The universe had other ideas. Hurricane Sandy was bearing down on the East Coast and despite staying up all night calling the airlines to try and get the first possible flight out, I was forced to stay.

Here I was again, wanting to bolt; being loved but not being able to feel it, because I hadn't given consent to it; feeling unsafe even when all the evidence did not support that.

The days after I stayed at the retreat, a group of us discovered a beautiful labyrinth. We walked the path to the center and back out again – the very symbol of the choice I need to continually make to feel love and belonging – which is the decision to go into the center where love resides and back out again. To my friends, to *the Rowdies*.

What I have found is that my life is so much bigger when I make this choice. Ceasing to look for love from external resources has transformed my friendships and opened the path to relationships with people I never would have considered as friends. I have discovered that when I relinquish people of the job of liking me – a job they can never really fulfill anyway– it gives them the space and freedom to just be. And that is when mutual love can flourish.

Meadow DeVor
....

My daughter informed me today that she wants a new mom.

She thinks I'm mean. That I ruin things for her. That I make people leave her. That it's my fault she's hurting. And I so don't want to hear this.

I want her to love me. I want her to think I'm amazing. Funny. Loving. I want to tell her my story. About me. About us.

I want her to agree with my version.

I want her to *want* to be my daughter.

Ironic.

She wants a different mom.

And I want a different daughter.

This is what we do to each other. We hold the other responsible for our own confusion. We blame the other for what we think has gone wrong. We point fingers at each other instead of at ourselves.

She thinks that if I changed - she'd feel better.
I think if she changed - I'd feel better.

The truth is: She's allowed to not want me as a mom. She's allowed to think that her life would be better without me. She's allowed to think that I'm the cause of her suffering.

Millions of people think the same things about their mom. I used to be one of them.

This thinking never gave me a different mom, though. It never made my mom better. It never made her do what I thought she should do. It never made her stop doing what I thought she shouldn't do.

It just made me miserable.

I have a lot of compassion for the pain my girl is feeling. I know how awful it is to believe that story. And I know I won't be able to help her find relief from her own pain if I'm in a hurry to have her love me the way I want her to - for my own sake.

My job isn't to persuade her to believe that I'm a great mom. I can't convince her of that. Nor should I.

My job is to be her mom - whether she likes it or not. To allow her to be my daughter – just as she is. Without the extra mom-loving modifications that I'm asking for today.

My job is to relieve her of the impossible duty of making me feel good.

And to teach her how to do the same.

To love her. And to keep loving her. No matter what.

49

ROWDY UP

Feelings can't land on us. They can't be painted on us. Or given to us. Our feelings are not determined by things, people or events. They aren't determined by what other people say (or don't say). They are solely determined by our own thinking. By the story we tell ourselves. By the perspective we take. We are ultimately responsible for the way we feel - because we are the only ones that can determine what we believe.

Where am I fighting reality with this person?

Where am I wanting to change their behavior?

What "pay off" am I expecting from this struggle?

Is my expectation reasonable? Why or why not?

How can I be even more of myself in this situation?

_____

What emotions/feelings am I attributing to the other person/situation instead of to myself?

_____

What would it mean to trust myself in this situation?

_____

Where does the energy naturally lie?

_____

What is the path of grace and simplicity?

_____

Am I willing to be in this situation/relationship with an open heart?

_____

If so, what would it look like?

_____

What action arises from a place of love, inspiration and abundance?

_____

MEADOW DEVOR

Chapter 4
. . . .

A Rowdy knows that
happiness is a skill that
requires practice.

Piyusha Singh

My life was series of check marks. Good school - check. Right major - check. Good graduate school - check. Good job - check. I was the quintessential 'good girl' constantly looking for rules to follow. I believed if I just figured out the right set of rules and followed them I'd be happy, right? I thought happiness was something you magically received when you accumulated enough check marks in your life. There was only one problem. With each additional check mark I became more unhappy.

I decided the problem was that I wasn't going for the right check marks, I needed to figure out what *I* really wanted and not follow other people's rules . So I started figuring out what I wanted. New job - check. Good friends - check. Nice house - check. Loving husband - check. Bouncing baby boy - check. Money in the bank - check. Soon I had a really nice set of check marks. Ones that felt warmer, that I wanted, that were more 'me'. But happiness? Still elusive.

Then I decided it wasn't what you did on the outside that mattered. Yoga, meditation, therapy, reiki, tarot, coaching. And they all worked...for a while. Sometimes I felt great after yoga, sometimes I didn't. Sometime meditation really helped me calm my mind, but sometimes it didn't. But I figured it wasn't what I was doing, it was me – I wasn't Zen enough, calm enough, spiritual enough.

By the time I met *the Rowdies* I was convinced that the best that one could hope for was a life of intermittent happiness, that depended on...what? No idea. The sun, the moon, the stars, a magical happiness fairy or maybe a butterfly fluttering its wings in South America. If all of that aligned it was a good day, if not it wasn't. Even worse, I had this knot of fear in my stomach. Besides a few broken hearts and disappointments I had been extremely fortunate in being able to get the check marks I chased. I had started playing small, not taking any risks, never going for anything I really wanted. Unwilling to risk failing to get anything that really mattered.

Becoming a Rowdy taught me that happiness is a skill. One you practice everyday. That you choose happiness. That you create the feeling - not your circumstances, not some check marks and certainly not the magical happiness fairy. I'm not going to lie - it really pissed me off at first. I didn't want happiness to be something I worked on, I wanted it to be something that someone else gave me. Forever. Once I reached the magical land of happy it was going to stay that way. What was all this practicing bullshit? Sounded like work. I refused to do it. *The Rowdies* patted my back and said "Um huh. Now go do your work." I dragged my feet, did everything but do the work and whined about how unhappy I was - and *the Rowdies* listened, supported and told me to go do the work.

Eventually I did. Grudgingly. Convinced it wasn't really going to make a difference. And I did it again the next day. And the next. After a while I noticed that I found my way to happiness and peace more often than not. I realized that happiness was something that I could practice. That it came from a way of thinking and being, and not from a set of circumstances in my life. As that realization sunk in, I noticed a bigger change. I stopped playing small, I stopped worrying about not getting the next check mark, I stopped worrying about wanting because I knew that my happiness didn't depend on wanting the right things or getting them – which freed me up to want things without attachment and to take the risk of moving towards something without needing a guarantee of success. As I write this piece I'm facing the fact that my infertility journey has come to an end without getting what I want – another child. This check box is going to remain unmarked. Two years ago the thought of moving on from here would have been unthinkable. Now I know that I can, and be happy doing it.

Bettina Ende-Henningsen

Seriously – happiness is a skill? Isn't happiness a destiny – something that fate delivers to your doorstep, something that "happens"?

If happiness is a skill, then for the last twenty years this skill seemed completely out of my reach. I thought that depression was my normal state of being. I felt spiritless, powerless, trapped and unable to act. I hated my body. Life felt like a burden, the days seemed unbearably long, the hands of the clock wouldn't move. I thought that I did not deserve happier moments.

If happiness is a skill that requires practice – how do you learn it? Can you go to happiness school? Take a happiness class? Do happiness homework?

Yes, yes, and yes again.

It's a matter of the right learning tools, a teacher who shares her insights, and a space for regular practice. This is what the Rowdy philosophy is about.

Learning and practicing are not new to me. I have learned languages, musical instruments, dancing, and my profession. I am finding out that learning happiness is not at all different from acquiring those other skills:

1. You start small – by turning around one single thought. It does not have to be good. It does not have to be pretty. You just tentatively strike that one key, balance on that foot for a second, try to pronounce that one word. For example, the thought "I'm unable to keep my weight stable" could be changed into the more neutral thought "My weight has been fluctuating a lot, lately."

2. You do your warm-up exercises – by turning your thoughts around in multiple ways, even playfully, until you have attained that degree of flexibility. You ask yourself what feels good, what feels better, what feels worse? ("I'm unable to keep my weight stable. - My weight has been fluctuating. – I have experienced changes in my body. – My body has adapted to different kinds of situations. – My body has an inner wisdom of its own.")

3. Persistence matters. You come back to your exercises day after day. For example, sitting down with pencil and paper every day, you will notice slight shifts in your relationship with your body. They will gradually lead you to a more contented place.

4. Truth is crucial. The good teacher will give you honest feedback. Your fellow *Rowdies* will give you tough love. Sometimes, you will learn the hard way. You will be hearing

things you don't like, but those are the ones you will learn the most from.

5. Secondary sources are helpful. Other people have gone this way before you. Many have documented their journeys. The universe is abundant with learning resources.

6. Multiple examples are essential. Our brain is prepared to learn. It loves to learn. There is nothing it can do better and is more willing to do. Fed with enough learning material, our brain is eager to find the patterns and create those happier paths and networks.

Last not least – it takes time. When we begin this practice, we expect our life to turn around very quickly. Then, we inevitably get to the point where we think that the changes are not happening fast enough. But honestly – I had practiced depression for twenty years, until I had become quite the expert. Happiness deserves the same patience.

Meadow DeVor

I need a helmet.

This isn't the first time I've said this.

And no, don't get excited, this isn't for motocross. Cycling.

Snowboarding. Football. Rapelling. Combat. Or anything else that might make me seem cool.

I need a helmet.

For yoga.

And for the record, they don't make one. I checked.

Here's the deal. I have a goal: I want to be able to do a handstand. Without a wall. Like. As in. Holding myself in perfect balance. Upside down.

I realize that I could have a perfectly satisfying life without ever accomplishing this mission. I could probably go for months. Maybe even years without the need for this talent.

The skill is actually pretty useless in real life.

But I still want to do it.

I've been practicing yoga for about 14 years. Handstands come up every so often. And I've always made either a half-assed attempt.

(Picture downward dog pose and add a flailing donkey kick.) Or I've used a wall.

(Picture downward dog pose with a really fast flailing donkey kick that propels me until I hit a wall. Hard. And then I fall back down.)

Shut up. It's pretty.

Ok. So... my yoga teacher doesn't really like either of these techniques. He actually puts his hands on the floor and his two feet seriously levitate into the air. I'm pretty sure his hands aren't even touching the ground.

He's just hovering. Upside down. Ok, not really.

But his handstands are bad ass. And I want to be bad ass too.

That's when I realized that I had never even considered that I would do a handstand.

This is what handstand used to sound like in my mind: Yah yah yah... I know ... blah blah-donkey-kick-blah. Let's move on.

This is what it sounds like now: Woah. I might really be able to do this. I'm going to practice. I'm going to get better.

This makes a lot sense - since I actually teach this shit. I teach that life is a practice. That happiness is a practice. That it's a skill that you can learn. And that you actually have to believe that you will do something before you will do it.

Kinda like handstand.

If you give a flailing-donkey-kick-attempt at a good life. That's about what you'll get. A donkeyish life. (I know. Profound right?)

You actually have to commit. Practice. And risk falling. Over and over.

It's a fine concept. I highly suggest it.

So over the past few months - I've been practicing. For reals.

And after about 100 full-assed attempts - I've started to kick up with serenity.

And then come down.

There's not really balance yet. But it's somewhat graceful. I'm getting better. And all of a sudden a handstand seems within my reach.

Which takes me to yesterday. I'm going through my practice.

And the teacher says. Kick up to handstand.

And I did. And I stayed.

And I was still up there.

And my feet were together.

And then.

I totally freaked out.

I felt like I was going to fall. And not in a good way. I thought about leaning to the right. But there is a wall of frail old windows that I really wasn't looking forward to plummeting through.

I thought about rolling into a somersault. But my beautiful MacBook Pro would be in the path of destruction.

(No silly. I wasn't doing email from my mat. I was taking an online class.)

So I did the only thing logical.

I dropped on my head.

With gusto.

Completely missing my yoga mat.

Spanish tile. Meet Meadow's skull.

This is what I learned... (Besides the fact that the health of my computer takes priority over the well-being of my noggin. Perhaps something worth looking into.)

Falling doesn't kill me.

It hurt. Don't get me wrong.

I've got a helluva lump on my head and a big bruise on my hip. But I'm alive.

All those flailing donkey kicks were preventing me from this moment. Knowing that I can take a risk.

And that I might fall. And that falling hurts. And that after I fall. I can get back up. Put on my helmet. And try again.

We can allow the fear of failure to stop us.

We can allow the pain of falling to stop us.

But you and I both know.

We're better than that.

ROWDY UP

Reality has no story. It presents itself as neutral until our mind gets involved. Practicing happiness means disciplining our mind. It's about disengaging from our reactions to our habitual thoughts. We do this by questioning our stressful stories and deliberately choosing to focus on a truer and kinder perspectives.

One uncomfortable feeling that I'm experiencing right now

_____

How would I rather feel right now? (Name the emotion.)

_____

What belief is preventing me from feeling that way?

_____

Is that belief true?

_____

Is it useful?

_____

Is it kind?

_____

Am I willing to surrender this belief in order to create my preferred feeling?

_____

What would I have to believe to create the feeling I'm wanting?

_____

List five reasons this new belief is truer.

_____

Practice tip: Continue searching for more evidence to support your new belief and to continue creating your desired emotion.

Chapter 5
. . . .

A Rowdy knows that peace can be found in any situation no matter how difficult.

Susan McCusker

I put off writing about this for weeks. Waiting for the moment when a joyful burst of love wrapped itself around me and I could wax poetic for 700 words about the wonders and virtues of love. The kind of love that holding a precious baby in your arms can inspire. The kind of love that watching your two best friends get married can inspire. The kind of love that is breathtaking in its beauty and hope.

But this is not that story. This story is brash and ugly. And very, very angry.

It is day eight of his detoxification and he has shut me out. I am left banging on the door for which I do not have a key. He has chosen to fight his battle alone. Without me. Without anyone.

I want to rail against this. Screech my anger and anxiety into the world. Watch it wrap around the house like thick, black rope, slowly strangling everything inside. I want to stop feeling like my own skin is peeling off me inch by painful inch, with a heat so searing that it makes me lose my breath.

His battle is his own. But so desperately do I want him to make it both of ours that I stand, stripped of everything, banging on the door. The door which he does not answer. The door he does not want me at. The stinging truth of that is like a whip across my back. I have a hundred rejoinders for him: let me in, let me help, let me fix you, I know what you need better than you do.

But most of all, this nakedness of mine is selfish. This is my own detoxification in a way. For the first time in a long while, it's not all about me. Not about my need to be loved, protected, cosseted, amused, entertained. To be saved. He is not capable of any of these things tonight; so mired in the withdrawal of his own addiction that he can only allow his heart to beat for one right now. It cannot beat for both of us. He is facing down his own demons. More than anything I want to stand with my sword at the ready, have his back, fight alongside him. But he won't allow it and this shatters me.

I pray. Meditate. Practice my breath. But all I can feel in my body is the burning grip of panic. A big red flame of fear and ugliness that is nestled right below my heart and ribcage, and it seems to expand with each breath I take. It has unfurled its tentacles tonight. The evenings are the hardest and eight days into this, my patience has reached its end. I step out onto my deck. Watch the sunset, the sky splashed with blue and pink. But this offers me no calm either. The ball of anger still pulsates and screams, "Love me. Love me. Love me. Let me in."

Somewhere in the blaze of my insides, a fine mist seeps in and squelches some of the flames. It is not enough to put out the fire, but it opens the tiny peepholes of possibility which gently blow across my angry flushed cheeks. A calming mantra gathers in my sternum: You can still love him. You can still love him. You can still love him. I turn my cheeks to the breeze. Let it caress them and take a deep breath. And then another. And another. I am gulping in the air as I straddle the line between despair and hope.

I slide open the door from the deck and step back into my kitchen. I want to say I am renewed; full of hope and possibility, ready to embrace him despite his resistance. But that is not true either. I watch my hands chop the vegetables that will make his dinner. And I listen to my children playing in the room next to me. The fiery, suffocating anger has passed and in its place is a residual resentment.

But still there is the love. The choice to end my suffering. The choice to love him now. Maybe even better than ever before. Maybe even despite the door in my face. Maybe even because he wants a drink more than he wants my love.

Maybe even despite the fact that this may not end the way I want it to.

Yet I choose to love him anyway.

I choose this because I know that love is infinite; our most abundant resource. It pours out of every nook, cranny, crevice and crack. Pours down like the rain, to wash us, renew us, split us open and cleanse us. We may have been programmed to believe that it only exists in lightness, or in passion, in plea-sure or in joyful times. But if we drop the veil, we'll find it there next to us all the time. It does not need neat and tidy packages. Indeed, some of love's greatest moments come in ugliness and despair.

His battle is my reminder: There is never a shortage of love. Not even when we block the love from ourselves, or when we try to stop it. Not when we can't see it or believe it has for-saken us. Not even when the door gets slammed in our faces, locked, and barred. In our darkest hours, and our greatest mo-ments of despair, the love keeps right on coming. It is always there. Steady, stable, and waiting for the moment when we are ready to choose to receive it.

Jen Greer

This is embarrassing. Please don't tell anyone that I'm a certified money coach. Especially Meadow.

Or that I've been a Rowdy on and off since the beginning. A certified coach well before that.

You see, I'm looking for a job. And I realized tonight that my main motivation in looking for a job is so I don't have to think about it any more.

So that I don't have to think about finding a job, what kind of job to get, whether I'll make $8 or $80 or $800 an hour, what my husband thinks about me not having a job.

Or worry about the fact that I'm not making much money to speak of right now, going through our savings 'til there ain't none left, my husband leaving me because he's fed up with an inadequate, under-earning partner.

Just don't have to think about this whole work money mess situation at all.

What's the big deal? Why the secret?

Getting a job to get rid of my thoughts just won't work. Rowdies know this. Meadow teaches it.

If your thinking is driving you nuts, the only path to peace is questioning your thoughts. Perhaps exploring the emotions beneath them.

Otherwise it's like playing a never-ending game of Whac-a-Mole.

I kick butt at Whac-a-Mole. Won a three foot stuffed parrot at Circus World when I was 15.

It was a proud moment. But it didn't alleviate my suffering. Didn't erase my loneliness, boost my dangerously low self-esteem or bring me peace of mind.

Nor will getting a job alleviate my suffering. It will simply shift it from one mole to another.

From the "I need to get a job" mole and all the related thoughts, to the "I need to find the right job" mole and all the associated thoughts.

Let's follow this path.

I get a job. I feel great. Maybe even have a little peace of mind. "Hot diggity dog! I don't have to think about getting a job anymore!"

This lasts a day. Maybe a week. On the outside, it might even last a month. But I doubt it.

Then all the "this isn't the right job" thoughts start gathering steam. They may whisper at first. Before too long the volume has been turned up. Way up. Only this time the story goes like this...

I'm in the wrong job.

I have to find the right job.

I have to find my passion, my purpose.

My boss undervalues me.

I should have asked for more money.

With this thinking running through my mind day in and day out, it's no surprise when I quit one day. Believing that leaving will free up time and energy for me to find my passion, my purpose—the job I'm truly meant to have. The one that will allow me to breathe easily and be happy. A glowing halo will appear around my head and my husband will start leaving me poems and fresh organic roses on my pillow each morning before I wake.

But that's not what happens. Instead I start worrying about how I'm going to find my purpose. Looking for the book, the training, the coach, the magic pill that will finally tell me what I'm supposed to do with my life.

Before too long, I also become acutely aware that I don't have a job. Don't have an income. Now I've got two freakin' moles running through my life, driving me batty.

I know this cycle well. I've lived it a few times now. Each time gets a little easier. And still, it's not a ride I want to continue.

What's the alternative?

The only path to peace is to stop running. Stop reacting. Stand still.

Look those moles—aka thoughts—right in the eye.

Understanding, truly understanding, that these thoughts will follow me wherever I go until I am willing to lift them up and see what's underneath.

Understanding that getting a job will bring me income, but it will not bring me peace.

The only place that I can truly find peace is here. Now. In me, in this moment.

No where else.

Not in a job, not an income, not a passion, not a purpose.

Here.

Now.

The only place. The only way.

ROWDY UP

The antidote to any suffering is to allow reality to be as-is. To give our permission to the past to be what it was. To give our permission to the present moment to be what it is. To allow our future to be what it will be. Trying to change reality only creates suffering, stress and confusion. Peace can be found through accepting, rather than arguing, with reality.

Where am I resisting or arguing with the past?

_____

The present?

_____

The future?

_____

Am I willing to give my permission to the situation, feeling, event, issue to be as-is? If so, what would that experience be like?

_____

Am I willing to allow what has happened/what is happening/what will happen? If so, what would that experience be like?

_____

Where am I judging or comparing?

_____

Am I willing to drop the labels and the judgment? If so, what would that experience be like?

_____

Am I willing to choose love, gratitude or compassion here? If so, what would that experience be like?

_____

Where am I attaching or clinging to ideas, labels and/or things?

_____

Where am I expecting permanence or ownership?

_____

Am I willing to believe that there is plenty for everyone? If so, what would that experience be like?

_____

What do I need to set free?

_____

Chapter 6
. . . .

A Rowdy knows that love, life, and joy are unlimited resources.

Tara Simkins

I was headed across the parking lot for what must have been the thousandth time. My eyes were focused on the revolving hospital door a hundred yards ahead of me while my mind was focused on my son, Brennan, who was lying in his hospital bed four stories above me. We had packed up our family and our lives and traveled across the country almost 12 months earlier with our hearts focused on delivering to Brennan more time, more life.

This walk from my car to the hospital room was a daily pilgrimage from a life in an outside world with Brennan's two brothers to a life in an inside world with Brennan. I was always conscious that every, single moment in either of these two worlds was to be treasured, and none was to be wasted on the journey from car to hospital room.

This time, however, I noticed something different. A narrow path lined with boxwoods and crepe myrtles, veering off to the left, extending and rounding its way back to the main sidewalk. Why hadn't I noticed it before?

Making my way as fast as I could, I paused at the path's threshold. As if accepting an invitation into another world, I stepped off of the main sidewalk and ducked under the limbs of the young crepe myrtle trees onto the path. Each sapling greeted me bowing and bending heavy with its magenta blossoms, and I bowed a thank you in return. The narrowness and arch of the path increased my awareness of my steps, my breath, my time.

I turned my gaze upward to Brennan's window and promised, "This will just take a minute. I will be right there." Careful not to spill a single second, I returned my focus to the path and placed one foot in front of the other. Each step was a prayer. "Please, let him live." Right foot. "Please, let him live." Left foot. "He is only eight." Heel. "Please, let him live." Toe.

Slowly, my mind calmed. Unexpectedly, I felt the wind blow across my face. I heard the robin, which was nesting in one of the trees, sweetly sing its song. Time, as if newly discovered, was where it had always been, filling my cup, overflowing into my life.

That's when I heard the Rowdy voice within me, "Whatever his time is will be enough."

"Could that be true?" I dared to hope. Right foot. Left foot.

I emerged from the path's portal, lighter. My mind's tight grip on its focus softened. I made my way through the revolving door and up to the room. I considered the truth behind the enough-ness of whatever time Brennan might be given, of whatever time any of us might be given.

Over the next ten months, I looked forward to my daily pilgrimage, and I watched as the strength and courage behind this voice and this thought about time grew within me while the young crepe myrtles grew alongside of me.

Discovering *the Rowdies* was like discovering this path, an unexpected oasis during a time in the desert. A community of women full of life who offered another way, a way focused on the journey we all share together rather than our arrival on that unknown, distant shore; a way *brimming* with inquiry and life and love; a way to experience the fullness, the boundlessness and the timelessness of our lives.

Every day as a Rowdy, the voice within me grows and grows. Every day as a Rowdy, I witness this voice growing in others. We do not walk this path alone. We walk it together, as Rowdies, each of us listening, "This time, our time, is enough. This time, our time, is full of life, goodness and abundance. This time, our time, is always available to us."

And to you.

ROWDY UP

Love isn't something we create. It isn't something that we need to protect or hold dear. It's something that we tap into. It is the essential life energy. Some might call it God. It's something that we must open our hearts to and give freely. When we live in an abundance of love, we clearly see that there are infinite moments in every hour and that each of those moments provide us with an unlimited expression of joy.

The amount of love that I can share is unlimited because

_____

The amount of love that I can experience is unlimited because

_____

The amount of love that I can receive is unlimited because

_____

Love is unlimited because

_____

The meaning of my life is unlimited because

_____

The purpose of my life is unlimited because

_____

The experience of my life is unlimited because

_____

My life is unlimited because

_____

The amount of joy that I can share is unlimited because

_____

The amount of joy that I can experience is unlimited because

_____

The amount of joy that I can witness is unlimited because

_____

Joy is unlimited because

_____

Chapter 7

. . . .

A Rowdy loves her body.

Wendy Kaufman

Cheetos, salty, orange, crunchy. Shredded wheat cereal coated in hard powdered sugar. Crumbly pretzels eaten straight from the bag. While standing up. And reading. Crumbs would fall everywhere, and I would hope the dog would find them later so I wouldn't have to clean them up.

This is how I lived and ate for almost 20 years. Whenever I arrived home from school, work, going out, a party, the ritual would begin. The standing-in-the-pantry-or-refrigerator-searching time. Searching for the hit to calm my stomach back down, calm my mind back down, bring me back to...nothing. The endless searching in a bag or a box for the salty, the sweet, the back and forth of both. The licking of the fingers, the subtle shift from pain into complete zoning out, oblivion, where all that mattered was where the next fix was coming from.

And this ritual was married to the even more sinister ritual of habitual dieting. The promise of a new diet was a reason to do something, to be someone, to get up in the morning and hope that "this" would be the answer to the mess of my eating life. To the mess of my emotional and spiritual life.

The diets would range from obsessive calorie counting, to cutting out food groups, to seeing "experts" in the field, and hoping that would be enough to break the addiction.

It wasn't.

And, finally, eventually, thankfully, I hit bottom. I stared at the scale in my nutritionist's office in disbelief the week after Thanksgiving. Weighing the most I'd ever weighed and wondering when I would stop using Cheetos and South Beach as distractions from myself. I thought I was doing everything right – I mean, I was even seeing a nutritionist for crying out loud! But, as I've been reminded so many times, the body never lies. And my body was telling me a truth I finally could see. I was using food and dieting as an escape from living my real life.

And, so, with bravery, with boldness, and with Rowdiness, I knew the only way out was through. And so I started unwinding the shit in my head that was in there that made the fix so appealing. And what was in there were stories. Made up stories of people against me, people hating me, the world setting me up to fail, society creating lack so I would have to suffer. Everything and everyone against me. Yeah, like that. Ugly awful stuff I wouldn't wish on anyone. I got my degree in Drama for a reason! So no wonder I wanted it all to go away. No wonder a packet of saltines, chocolate malt balls, and nachos with extra fake yellow cheese sauce were more appealing to me than living my life.

Slowly I began to unravel those stories. To question them. I learned how to ask myself what was true, what was false, and how I felt when I thought that way. I learned how to turn around the thoughts that I believed. I started meditating. For three minutes a day on my little purple meditation cushion. And many times, by doing that, I set my mind straight for the rest of day. I practiced yoga. Sometimes just sitting on my mat and breathing would be enough to bring me back to connection with myself. Sometimes it took a really long walk and a whole weekend of patience.

Our physical health is a manifestation of what is happening on the inside. In our minds, with our emotions, with our innermost voices that speak to us in whispers, in dreams, in fleeting twinges in the body. Meadow always talks about how our bodies never lie, how they reveal what is actually going on underneath the surface.

And extra weight and obsessive dieting, for me, were an indicator of that internal stress, anxiety, insecurity. All bundled up into one neat, fat package.

I was fat for twenty years. Some of the fat was because I chose the wrong foods for me in the wrong portions. And most of the fat was because I didn't feel good. And the way I ate matched the way I felt.

I learned that hot fudge sundaes are wonderful, and so are nachos and chocolate malt balls, but they are substitutes for the real thing. The real thing can't be sold in a package or squirted in a bowl. The real thing is getting real. The real thing is telling the truth. To myself. In my mind. In the way I see the world. And nothing is sweeter than the truth.

I would rather question my stories, unravel my anxieties, and understand how my mind spins things, than eat. Learning to live in a way that connects to truth and to love was what I have always wanted. And *the Rowdies* help me connect back to that when I forget.

I connect in daily now. I have learned how to question the pain. I have a group of women that will gently show me that pain and lead me back to truth. I have guides in my life that have lit the way back for me. To home. To a home that still loves drama but on a much smaller screen, playing in the background. On mute most of the time.

Susan Loucks

"I'm going to be 40 in 102 days." I was unsure about what the number meant. And afraid that I would get busy and I wouldn't be physically or mentally ready. I had struggled with my weight for so much of my life that it was ingrained in me. I was afraid that if I didn't have my shit together at 40 it will be all downhill from there. Losing 10 pounds became my fixation.

So I decided to count down. I tracked each day in my food journal- desperately trying to lose those 10 pounds. The count-down was designed to keep me aware of my timeline until the big day and instill a little bit of panic in me. Food journals are designed to create awareness, but they have no power without acceptance first. I tried berating myself. I tried bullying my-self. I tried criticizing myself. None of it worked.

I spent a ton of time trying new eating plans, new workouts, al-ways reaching to be just a bit leaner. Trying to keep my weight under control. To feel in control. I looked at myself through a distorted lens which had created a long history of poor body image and weight struggles.

By the time I reached my birthday, a piece of me had been surrendered. I started seeing the fixation with the scale as trivial and meaningless. I started to find beauty in life. In myself. And I began to let go of the ridiculous story of how my thighs should look. It was clear to me that now was the time to change. I woke up to the fact that I am not overweight, I do not need to go to "weight school". I have so much good in my life and I just need to love it all and be thankful for me just as I am. I spend a lot of time loving other people and not enough time loving myself.

What I thought I wanted for my 40th birthday was to lose ten pounds. But what I really wanted was to just feel comfortable in my own skin. To like the way I look. To appreciate my body. The gift of self love. This gift was not one that comes with a bow or a price tag - it comes through the hard work of forgiveness and acceptance. It comes through the surrender of the fantasy that you've been holding a torch for. It comes from deliberately choosing to love yourself - rather than belittle yourself.

On the morning of my birthday I got the most wonderful messages from *the Rowdies*. Not a single Rowdy wished me thinner thighs, leaner arms or to a size 6 for my birthday. They reminded me what is truly important. They wished me happiness. Joy. Peace. Family. Connection. Friendships. Love. And I continue to practice loving and accepting myself every day.

Now instead of constantly comparing and judging my body I am listening to it. If it says slow down, I slow down. When I look in the mirror, I am so much less judgmental. I look at my full hips and not so thin thighs and arms and am grateful for a healthy body. I am more accepting. I am not constantly comparing myself to others anymore. I am not always thinking that someone else is better, prettier, thinner and I should be different. I look at people now with a sense of wonder about how different we all are physically and how boring it would be if we all looked the same. The physical attributes that used to be so important to attain and live up to have taken a back seat to being mentally happy, kind to myself, and growing my mind not my biceps. There is daily work to be done here, but I feel like I am more mindful of my thoughts and so much more kind to myself now.

They say life begins at 40. For me love, whole-hearted love, begins at 40. And I was the most awesome me I could be at 40. Not thinner, smarter, prettier, better. Just me. Rowdy me.

ROWDY UP

We must learn to love the body. We have to practice appreciating the vehicle that travels us through our lives. Flaws and all. Only through love and acceptance will we be able to truly care for our body. Sometimes we are afraid of allowing ourselves to love the imperfect. As if this means that we are lowering our standards. Or that we are terminally giving up hope. It's the exact opposite. To truly change - we must learn to love where we are. Right now. What we look like right now. To accept and care for the body that we have in this moment.

Where am I fighting reality with my body?

_____

Where/how have I betrayed my body?

_____

What "pay off" am I expecting from keeping struggle with my body?

_____

Is my expectation reasonable? Why or why not?

_____

How can I be even more of my higher self in this situation?

_____

What emotions/feelings am I holding my body responsible for?

_____

What would it mean to trust my body in this situation?

_____

What would it mean to trust the universe (God or my higher self) in this situation?

_____

*Where would the path be if I followed the natural wisdom of my body?
What is the path of grace and simplicity?*

_____

How can I practice offering care and healing?

_____

*Am I willing to have an open heart in my relationship with my body?
If I am, what would that look like? If not, why not?*

_____

What action arises from a place of love, inspiration and abundance?

_____

Chapter 8

. . . .

A Rowdy loves her money.

Ivonne Senn

The motorbike turns onto the street and I watch it until it disappears behind a corner. It takes all I've got not to jump into my car and follow him, to tell him that together we will find another solution, which usually means I will force money on him so that he doesn't have to endure any kind of emotional pain. Yes, for many years I really thought I had the power to make somebody else feel better. I mean, why else was I wearing this cape if not to rescue my husband whenever he didn't ask for it?

Then I met Meadow. 'Sit down and relax,' she said. 'But I can't,' I replied. 'I am on duty. Can't you tell I'm Supergirl?' I pointed to my cape, but when I looked at it, all I saw was a tightly woven cloth of false beliefs dragging behind. And all of a sudden I felt its weight, felt how it pulled me down and under, how I had to struggle to keep staying upright. It was not me who dragged the cloth forward, it was the cloth that held me back. 'What can I do to make this go away?' I asked.

The woman had one question for me.

'What did your family teach you about money?'

The answer to this question was the beginning of unraveling the cloth and uncovering my hidden beliefs about me, my life and money.

'What did my family teach me about money?' That earning a lot of money is good. That being rich is bad. And my financial life represented both of these beliefs. Being a people pleaser at heart and also extremely ambitious, I had made many fortunes but prevented myself from being rich by spending more than I had ever made.

'Who is the most important person in your life,' was the second question the wise redhead asked me.

Hm, who is it. What should I say? Parents, sister, husband? As soon as I thought one name I instantly felt disloyal to the others. A feeling that intensified when I finally realized who it not yet was, but who it should be.

Me.

I am the most important person in my life. Ouch. That went against all I was taught about not being selfish. But if it weren't for me, my life would not exist. I need to take care of myself before I can take care of someone else. Financially. Emotionally.

Instantly the cloth lost another couple of inches. I caught a glimpse of a living, breathing picture of my past. My younger self, still unaffected by other people's expectations. A girl who loved money. A girl who always had enough money. A girl who trusted that she is enough just the way she is. A girl who knew that nobody needs to be saved – not even by her.

I wanted to be the grown-up version of this girl. I started to write my own story about money. It is going to be a real love story. With a strong heroine, kitschy sunsets and a happy ending. And so I am standing here watching my husband drive away on his bike which he is going to sell for his dream of building a company. It still takes a lot not to hastily paint the Supergirl logo on the old cloth and rush to his rescue. But by now I know better. He deserves to gain his own experiences. I take one deep breath and turn my back to the window. Supergirl has grown up. She calls herself Rowdy now.

Kira DeRito

In November of 2010 I signed on to work with my first money coach, the amazing Meadow DeVor. I felt broken; scared and furious with myself nearly every moment of the day for the actions I'd taken that resulted in my exceptionally weak financial position. I was pretty sure that I wouldn't be able to help myself without getting some sort of handle on where I stood, but I was too afraid of what I would find to look on my own. What I knew for sure was that my accounts and numbers were dripping red. I didn't know what was on my credit report, I didn't know how much debt I had, and I didn't even know exactly who I owed because my debts had been repeatedly sold. I didn't know these things on purpose. I had willingly stepped inside a financial jail and refused to let myself out. Every late fee and shut off notice added another month to my sentence. I was *guilty*, and when I wasn't scheming to figure out how to borrow more money, I dreamed of a full pardon via a winning lotto ticket or random inheritance. I wanted someone to save me, and I wanted to feel good all of the time. I didn't want to get out of debt – I wanted to have gotten out of debt. No hard work, please. The instant gratification siren song of the original Hot Mess Emotional Child: me.

Meadow held my (virtual) hand and told me the truth. Learning to love money (for real) was the key and my struggle was the *cause* of my overspending and under–earning, not the solution. Through careful examination of my individual thoughts around all aspects of money, I developed the ability to set down the struggle and find a way to the result I wanted (financial health) through a much more effective path of kindness and love.

Here are a few things I learned while working with Meadow and *the Rowdies*. (And of course this is an on-going process – I learn and relearn and forget and learn again. Much like one visits the gym on a regular basis to keep a body healthy; I hang with Meadow and *the Rowdies* to keep my mind and thoughts healthy.)

1. Money does not equal freedom. It's easy to see why I believed that money meant freedom – it appears to make sense and easily masquerades as the truth. If you've ever had anyone hand you unexpected cash, it's a certain flavor of giddiness that leaves you hungry for more. For most of my life I thought it was the cash that gave me that special giddy, that taste of freedom, that possibility. What I learned is that the cash itself is neutral. It's paper. It's simply a story that we, as a society, have all agreed to believe. And not until I apply a thought to the paper in my hand does it transform into freedom. Yes, it is *much* easier to slide into a thought that creates the feeling of freedom when I'm holding a lot of paper. But easier is not fact. Easier is not truth. It's just easier. When I learned that I could feel free simply by *thinking* free, I began to understand that freedom was

available to me at any time, in any circumstance, with any amount of money. And that was True Freedom.

2. I can do hard things. The fact of the matter is that I was *doing* hard things repeatedly, every day, and getting myself further and further away from what I said I wanted. It's okay that it is hard. It's okay that it's not fair. Arguing with reality and wanting things to be 'easy' was actually the more difficult, off-the-tracks way of getting my financial train over the debt hill. (Or, in my case, *not* getting over the debt hill.) Accepting what is true as truth got me to an internal place of grace and back on track. My money train still had to get over that debt hill, but now the effort that I was expending *anyway* was targeted in a way that got me to my destination – Cash City.

3. I started with wanting and loving what I had. I was mad at my business for not being more profitable, I was disappointed in my husband for not providing a magical fountain of money, and I was disgusted with myself for everything. A simple practice of intentionally and purposefully wanting and loving what I already had cranked the dial on my creativity and released frustration and resentment. From that place my options became much more obvious and I was able to identify that I (surprise!) wanted what I had. At that point, I was able to build.

4. Loving money is where the magic is. When I love something, *I pay attention* to it. When I first started this process I learned to think of money as a beloved pet. It matters to me where it goes and what it does. It matters to me where it came from. I give it room to run and I don't try to get rid of it. I send it off to do its work in the world without resentment or fear or loss. I welcome it back. I tell it the truth and I don't pretend. I let it in and make a home for it. I wonder

what it's doing, and I make sure it is healthy.

Today, my financial picture looks limitless. I only have to decide what particular shade of color to dab on the canvas, and my view shifts. My business is strong, profitable and growing, I am intimately familiar with all of my numbers and I am debt free except for a financially intelligent mortgage. Life, is good. Meadow and the beautiful women of Rowdyville have helped me develop the beliefs that not only have produced my current state of abundance, but also help me to know that if life ever hands me lemons, I will make (and sell for a tidy profit) lemonade. If all my money disappeared tomorrow, I would still have the privilege and pleasure of knowing that 'The Bank' is actually my mind and the specific, deliberate thoughts I choose to practice. No matter what is "out there," on the inside there is always plenty of money in 'The Bank.'

ROWDY UP

Our relationship with money is not a frivolous thing. Money is a force in our life, whether we like it or not. Our relationship with money isn't determined by luck or by chance. It's determined by our beliefs. Our beliefs about our worth. Our worthiness. The work that we do in this world. And about the things that we value. Loving money means being at peace with money. Being proud of the money we earn. Being conscious of the money we spend. And living with integrity and honoring our financial commitments.

Where am I fighting reality or struggling in my financial life?

_____

What "pay off" am I expecting from keeping this struggle with money?

_____

Is my expectation reasonable? Why or why not?

_____

Where/how have I betrayed my money?

_____

How can I be even more of my higher self in this situation?

_____

What emotions/feelings am I holding money responsible for?

_____

What would it mean to trust money in this situation?

_____

What would it mean to trust the universe (God or my higher self) in this situation?

_____

How can I practice offering care and healing?

_____

Am I willing to have an open heart in my relationship with my money? If I am, what would that look like? If not, why not?

_____

What action arises from a place of love, inspiration and abundance?

Chapter 9

· · · · · · · · · · · · · · ·

A Rowdy knows that love comes from the inside out.

Meadow DeVor

I said a prayer for my heart tonight.

I felt that cold seeping in.

The inky blackness that hides in my veins. Just waiting for a call to duty. To harden and cement a barrier so thick that I will be protected from this hurt.

The white–hot barbed-wire that courses from my gut. Twisting and turning a tangled rusted knot. Weaving itself a corset through my rib cage. Suffocating and stifling. Tighter. Till there were only two words.

Love me.

The two words that risk the most dangerous of dangers:

To love and to be rejected.

And I know rejection.

I know what it's like to have your mother call you a pig. Rip off your clothes. And make your brother and sister watch while she whips you with the belt buckle.

I know what it's like to have your father fear you more than he can ever love you.

I know what it's like to have a man leave you. But not all at once because that would just be too kind. Instead, it's in millimeters and moments. Till you don't quite remember if he was ever there in the first place.

I know rejection.

And still. I hear the words.

Love me.

I want to obliterate them. Banish them from my memory.

I want to shut them up. Gag them. I want to puke them out. And flush them away. I want to hide them somewhere safe. For some other night when I will know that I can trust.

And still. My soul will not be silenced. It craves connection. It speaks that moon language.

It knows the truth. That love is never dangerous.

So I said a prayer for my heart tonight.

And my tears washed the blackness away. And the ocean wind broke through the weathered barbed-wire.

And I remembered.

The two words that repair all wounds.

And keep any heart from turning to stone.

I remembered the two words that obliterate all risk. All danger.

The two words that make me willing to walk out into this dark night. Alone. And not afraid.

I love.

The two words that remind me that it's not about what I get back. It's not about being accepted, approved of, or included. It's not about how well I can contort myself to fit your expectations. It's about what I give. To you. To me. To all of us.

I love.

Because it's not worth living life any other way.

And even though the hardening and steel sing their siren song seducing me toward their fortressed prison.

I shut my eyes tight.

And say a prayer for my heart.

To help it choose to love.

Because this is the only direction to keep walking.

Wendy Kaufman

Lying in his bed in steamy New Orleans, his orange cat purring inches from my face, making biscuits on my soft belly. Her towel with the initials S.O. hanging on the empty canopy rack. He still uses her fucking towel?!

I reach for the Marlboro Red pack in my crumpled jeans and light up. 6:42 A.M. Two hours of sleep. That's ok, we can do this. We're gonna drive home, we're gonna wait tables, we're gonna get through this. All is well now that I got my hit of candy man. I walk through the apartment. Pieces of her everywhere still left behind. He never bothered to replace the curtains she yanked from the bedroom window so the sun blared through the apartment like a spotlight, illuminating dust particles and cigarette smoke. His needles in the bathroom drawer I would so conveniently ignore.

You are up to no good! What the hell do you think you're doing? You're so not supposed to be doing this! What are you doing? And yet, that question would make me smile with glee at my rock star life.

Driving home, I am so tired, I can barely concentrate on the five mile drive. Stop at crosswalk, peer at children in school uniforms and crossing guards. God, I am such a slut. How can these seemingly normal people be up and about and go on with life?

Tonight there will be Mardi Gras parades two blocks from my house. For lunch, I'll shove down some king cake, fill up a plastic cup with bourbon and diet coke, and throw on some beads. Make sure my tank top is nice and tight. Better not eat dinner, better suck it in all night. Maybe he'll like me better if I am thinner, sexier, funnier, more alive.

And yet. He doesn't. He'll tell me he loves me, but he can't be with me. He'll tell me he needs me, yet he won't be there when I'm sick. And I'll move away, and that will be the last I'll hear of him.

All good drugs wear off eventually. The rock star life comes with a price. The price of knowing that the boys don't really love you because you don't love yourself. You're using them as much as they're using you.

Parade's over. Summer's come again. It's time to move on. That sun was too bright anyway.

It's time to Rowdy up.

Find out what makes me tick. Find work I might love. Find a way to be of service. Find out how to pray. Find out how to give. Find out how to move out of my head. Find out how to be a real friend and find real friends back.

I had been drowning in a sea of beads, sugar and diet coke.

Because that boy would never, could never love me meant that I had to find that inside. Because now I was out in the world, done with school, done with being cared for, I had to care for myself. And I wasn't ever going to be seduced by parades again.

When I arrived home to California, bourbon still on my breath, I had my suitcase and nothing else. I had to create a life.

I know it was my inner Rowdy that brought me home. And taught me that the rock star life is even better lived in your own bed. As your own best friend. And self respect at your side.

ROWDY UP

The desire for love, appreciation, approval or acceptance is a foolproof way to create suffering. Because desiring something that no one else can create for us leads to endless heartache. No one can make us feel loved, or make us feel appreciated, or approved of, or accepted without our own consent. These are feelings that we can only create for ourselves. We can end the suffering by cultivating and taking responsibility for our desired feelings and by stopping the addictive and painful cycle of wanting external validation.

I love the sound of

_____

I love the taste of

_____

I love to talk to

_____

I love to read

_____

I love to see

_____

I love to go to

_____

I love to feel

_____

I love to smell

_____

I would love to hear

_____

I would love to see

_____

I would love to touch

_____

I would love to smell

_____

I would love to taste

_____

Chapter 10
. . . .

A Rowdy knows that vulnerability is strength, that vulnerability is beautiful

Susan McCusker

I want to cook.

Or maybe clean.

Possibly take a shower.

Or plan a vacation.

Even go to the dentist or doctor, maybe both on the same day.

Anything rather than this.

I have an idea. A big idea. An idea that could really launch my business into something great. And I am absolutely petrified. I am so scared, that I am almost motionless. I have already been through the first stage of processing this. I call it attempted denial. It's the pretense that my idea won't work, can't work, that I absolutely, positively, have NO time for this. That it's ridiculous.

But then a little voice inside me keeps pushing. Keeps suggesting gently that maybe I shouldn't give up yet. So here I am in the second phase, which I suppose you could call something pleasant, like acceptance. But which in fact feels like the complete opposite. It is resistance to acceptance. It is anger and fear. Writhing, like a fish on the end of a line, desperate to escape. Full of fury that I have to push myself down this road. Yet, also quietly knowing at the core of my heart that I am going to do this. Whether I want to or not, because something greater than my ego is on the line here and it won't just cut and let me go.

The thing I want to escape most is surprising to many people. It's not actually the fear of failing. It's not really the financial implication that my business may incur if this doesn't work. It's not even the worry that nobody will buy what I want to sell.

It's much more insidious than that.

What I am fighting against is the vulnerability that this idea requires: the need to put myself out there.The need to come out of hiding. We all hide. Many of us do it instinctually. We closet ourselves from the world, and push our deepest dreams and desires down as far as they will go. In a sense we're programmed to do this from the time we are children. Not to share too much of ourselves with the world, because it's a dark and devilish place. People will judge you. People will laugh at you.

Vulnerability may as well be a four-letter word.

But lately I am teasing the possibility that vulnerability is actually much less painful than hiding. That in the long run, being vulnerable, and sharing who I am with the world (in this case through my business) would feel like freedom. And kindness. And peace. Whereas hiding has gotten to be continually more difficult. Hiding requires suppressing my light. Hiding requires toeing the line. Hiding requires staying small. Because it's hard to hide something big and bold and bright.

The world needs vulnerability now, more than ever. In an age where we are able to document each and every moment of our lives, in text, pictures, posts, and tweets, one would assume that we are less hidden than ever before. But it's the opposite really. The carefully constructed world of social media allows us to craft an image of who we want to be, to hide the ugly stuff, the bad moments. Rather, we live vicariously through other people's posts and pictures. Or even worse, feel like we have to compete with them. The hiding that is required in this kind of world is exhausting. And overwhelming. And never-ending.

So here I sit, wondering what would happen if I gave wings to my business idea. Let it into the world, and set it free. To land wherever it might. Would people laugh? Maybe. Would they judge me? Almost certainly. Would that vulnerability kill me? Not likely. In fact, I think it's the very thing that will make me feel alive.

And with that, I quietly slip into the next phase. Taking action.

Jen Greer

I've written two pieces for the *Tao of Rowdy*. This is my third. Writing the first two pieces bore unexpected gifts. The gift of deep connection with myself. Seeing myself and life through new eyes. New ways of seeing that create greater freedom and space in my life.

The gift of deep connection with other beautiful Rowdies. Knowing them more intimately by sharing parts of me and by witnessing the way they generously give their tender selves over to the page.

I've had a blog for the past few years, and I write infrequently. So infrequently that next month will be a year since my last blog post. Ideas are not the issue. Years' worth of daily blogs float through my mind on a regular basis. With twenty years of professional writing and editing experience, skill is not the issue either.

I wrote the *Tao of Rowdy* pieces with ease and grace— yet my blog remains unwritten.

Writing for the *Tao of Rowdy,* I walk alongside other beautiful Rowdies as we create this book together. I believe this book will touch lives. It will be read.

I feel a little vulnerable. But the support of the other Rowdies and the belief that this book will touch lives makes this vulnerability tolerable. Uncomfortable, yet manageable. I have the image of being naked in a clan of beautiful naked women surrounded by people who lovingly adore us.

Take away *the Rowdies*, remove you - dear reader - and my imagination takes me to a different image. One where I'm simply standing naked, cold and alone in a coliseum, stands full of angry faces, stones in hand.

Now vulnerability feels life-threatening. No wonder I haven't blogged in a year.

I'm learning that I have this backwards. Avoiding vulnerability poses the real threat. If I live in hiding, avoiding the so-called dark parts of myself, avoiding sharing my truth with you, I will surely miss the life that's waiting for me.

I miss the opportunity to express myself through the blog, maybe through a book or even a movie. Miss the joy of creating. The joy of sharing. Miss the way my heart lifts when someone tells me that reading my story gave them hope where before they had none. I miss life's precious gifts. I miss my precious self. I miss the possibility of true connection with you.

Instead, I must turn and face the places I've been avoiding for years. Practicing this, I find discomfort. I find pain. But there's also relief. Relief in finally sitting with what's real. In finally sitting with the truth. In finally sitting with myself.

I have a choice. And so do you. I can choose the never-ending suffering that comes from avoiding myself and the dark places within. Or I can choose the temporary discomfort of the truth.

When I'm willing to turn toward myself and sit with the discomfort, I find what I've been after all along.

Beyond those dark places and around the shadowy corners, I find love. True connection.

The seeds of vulnerability.

If I turn and face you, with all my bent and broken bits no longer hidden away, I can truly see you. I give you the opportunity to see me.

When I truly stand in vulnerability, I stand in myself.

I stand naked, vulnerable, with you.

And even if you turn away from me, I now know that the love and connection I've found cannot be lost.

ROWDY UP

Vulnerability doesn't come from fear. It isn't weak. Vulnerability is fierce. Strong. And powerful. It is courageous. And open. It is the willingness to show up completely as ourselves. It is the heroic act of stepping into one's life with absolute ownership. It's the willingness to speak the truth about our beliefs, our feelings, our actions. It is the unwillingness to reject, shame and forsake the shadow–parts of ourselves. It is the trust of our whole-self. And it is the unwavering and profound sense of abiding stability that is found when we show up with humility, and in service, to mankind.

Five things I know to be true...

1.

_____

2.

_____

3.

_____

4.

_____

5.

_____

If you really knew me...

_____

You'd know that I love

_____

You'd know that I fear

_____

You'd know that I regret

_____

You'd know that I hope

_____

You'd know that I long for

_____

You'd know that I worry

_____

You'd know that I smile when

_____

Chapter 11
. . . .

A Rowdy lives a life of truth.

Pat Davenport

If you want to find out how important it is to live a life of truth, try living a life of lies.

For me, it was never a conscious thing. I didn't set out to live a life of lies. I was taught, from an early age, that it was my job to keep everybody else happy. If somebody was mad, it was my job to make it better. Stay below the radar and don't make waves. Go with the flow.

I carried this into my relationships. There was always a story – after his promotion, after he passes his boards, after he makes partner, then what I want will matter. It didn't. He wanted a divorce. He got it.

I re-entered the dating world with a very fragile sense of self. I found myself in another relationship where someone else's needs came first. I spent sweaty weekends working with him on his house so he could sell it in hopes that we could move forward. I worked for his business - without pay.

Told myself, "It's ok. This doesn't matter. My needs will come later."

They didn't. The relationship ended before we got to me.

I thought I had learned my lesson. I thought I finally knew better. That I wouldn't do *that* again. Then, a year later, I found myself in a new relationship. I walked on eggshells because his wife had died and he was going through a lot with his business.

I moved North for him. Even though, I hate the cold. I hate gray days.

First lie: I can live in the cold.

Second lie: This is what I have to do to have a relationship.

He said I'd be fine if I just "stayed busy."

Third lie: He knows what's best for me.

I was not taking care of myself.

Fourth lie: I'm not that unhappy.

Fifth lie: Yes, I want to sail across the Atlantic in November.

Anyone who knows me would not have believed it if you said I was going to sail, in winter, off the equivalent of the coast of Nova Scotia, in an unheated boat. They'd have laughed themselves silly, in fact. But there I was, basically camping in the cold for two weeks. I was beyond miserable, even hypothermic at times during the first two weeks of the trip.

And that's how I ended up, literally, at sea. On a boat. Hundreds of miles from land. Sick with an infection, burning with fever, close to death. Lying alone in a cabin, talking to God.

"Please, I've had enough. I'm ready."

I had gone on this last leg of the trip against my instincts.

Lie: I don't feel that bad.

Lie: He can't do it without me.

By the time it became obvious to my boat-mates that it was an infection and not seasickness, I was pretty far gone. I swallowed antibiotics, thinking it was probably too late.

I lay there quietly, ready to die.

The fever finally broke, and I was able to start taking in fluids. I didn't die.

Oh. Crap. That was it. Time to tell the truth. Putting myself last almost cost me my life. And I didn't want to do it any more.

Truth: I want to leave.

Truth: I want to see my doctor.

Truth: This is going to make waves. And that's ok.

Truth: The real issue is that there is a part of me, deep down, that thinks I have to be sacrificed for someone else's best interests.

Truth: I need to believe that I am important as well.

Truth: I want to walk a better path. One that looks at the truth. In every moment. The real truth about who I am, what I want, what I like and what I don't.

Truth: I need to start showing up 100% authentically. To tell the truth. And trust that I am worthy of love.

I had to let go of the lie that I had to "do something" to be loved. That I had to earn love. That I had to "be something" other than myself to be loved.

And this will be a life-long practice for me. Raising the bar for my self-love. Learning that I don't need to forsake myself. Learning that I can love myself and another.

To learn to live a life of truth.

ROWDY UP

Many of us have been taught to pretend. Justify. Fake it. Play nice. And the best that we can create with those skills? A pretend-nice life. To permanently change our lives, we have to be willing to open our eyes. To start telling the truth about our money, our body, our health, our career, our relationships. We need to take responsibility for our past and present behaviors. And, most importantly, we need to understand why we have created the reality in which we're standing - in the first place. The truth is the antidote to anxiety.

What does the truth mean to you?

_____

Are you living a life of truth? Why or why not?

_____

What truths aren't you telling?

_____

Who do you lie to most often?

_____

What truths are you afraid to admit?

_____

When is it difficult to tell the truth?

_____

When is it easy to tell the truth?

_____

Are you keeping secrets? Why?

_____

Chapter 12
. . . .

A Rowdy is committed
to being extraordinary.

Meadow DeVor

I have a question that I'd love for you to answer. Try not to read ahead quite yet. I want you to articulate your own answer to this.

What makes a person extraordinary?

What is it that makes up that extraordinary-ness?

What is your definition of a truly amazing human being?

Pause. Don't read on. Answer the question first.

Really think about it. Think about the people who you think are amazing or extraordinary.

I posted this question in Rowdyville, and what we found was a very simple two-step concept that sets apart Mother Teresa. Martin Luther King. Oprah. Or any other amazing person that you know.

1. They know who they are.
2. They live the life they truly want to live.

I am shocked at how utterly simple and crazy-difficult it is to be an amazing human being.

Step Number One is a doozy of a step. I tried to avoid this step for years. I knew(ish) who everyone around me was ... and I thought that just might be enough.

It's not.

Step Number One is intensely spiritual, soul-wrenching, life-opening work.

You can't rush it.

You don't really arrive at it. There are no "Know Yourself" flash cards or study guides. And you can't cheat off of someone else's test.

But at some point in your life you will be given the opportunity to find out who you truly are.

If you want to be an extraordinary human being - you must take this class.

Again and again.

Until you know all the answers by heart.

Maybe it's just me, but there's something about getting a divorce, losing all your money and sitting in a little room alone for months-on-end that kinda bangs this lesson into your head. (Maybe your road was easier than this - but you're probably not an ultra-stubborn red-head. Lucky you.)

So when you figure yourself out and finally know who the hell you are... awesome things start happening, right?

Not.

No angels come down to sing to you.

No waters part from the sea.

No double rainbows all the way.

Nope, now it's time to do the real work.

The work of going out and truly living the life you want to be living.

The work of your life.

And this doesn't mean 'do whatever you want' in a reckless, passive or stupid way. It doesn't mean start boozin', sexin', druggin', spending money, living-like-a-rock-star-with-a-death-wish.

It means to deliberately go out and do the thing that you want to do.

That thing that you know you need to do.

It means to go take those pictures in Morocco. Or learn to sail.

It means start that nonprofit.

Or have that baby.

Or get that divorce.

It means quit that job. And start to really tell the truth.

It means to do those things. Those things that seem so 'un-amazing' that they almost seem scary. Or boring. Or risky.

Step Number Two is a work in progress for me. But this idea has been an insightful tool. It a compass pointing true north.

And it guides me toward my most-amazing-self-ness.

There are a lot of ordinary people out there.

There are people who refuse to learn themselves.

There are people who are afraid to live the life they want to live. (If you call that living.)

And there are too many people who will die without having made the brave step toward their own amazing-ness.

I know that you're not one of these people.

Get to know who you are.

And then do the fucking work to live that life.

It's time.

ROWDY UP

We are not the roles we play. Or the labels we have. We are not our jobs, our rankings or our titles. All of those things can be taken away from us. We can lose the title of mother, wife, business owner, sister, friend. And what's left when those titles are stripped gets to the heart of who we really are. We are not what we do. We are what we love. What we live for. We are our desires and our truths. To discover this takes time and discipline and it requires us to stop identifying ourselves through our external labels. This work is the pre-requisite for extraordinary women. The work that sets us up to do the real work of showing up as ourselves and living the life that we love.

Who are you?

_____

I love...

_____

I believe...

_____

I know...

_____

I want...

_____

I don't like...

_____

I am willing to...

_____

I would die for...

_____

I live for...

_____

What life do you truly want to live?

_____

I want to be ...

_____

I want to do...

_____

I want to believe...

_____

I want to know...

_____

I want to love...

_____

I want to live...

_____

Chapter 13
. . . .

A Rowdy loves. Period.

Kristen Baker

I used to think love was safety. Protection. Taking care of each other. Responsible for each other. I used to think love was indebtedness. I used to think love was holding onto the other person tightly. Like life was a free fall, jumping out of an airplane, and only another person had my parachute. And I had to cling to them to survive. I thought love was being special. I thought love was only for the lovable, the worthy, the good enough. I thought these were states I could ebb and flow in and out of. Lovable sometimes, unlovable others.

I used to think love meant saving and being saved from pain. Leaning on someone meant collapsing into them. I used to think love required sacrifice. Even suffering. I used to think love meant sparing the object of love from pain. That there were objects of love. That love could be lost. That love had to be fought for. I had so many stories around love, so many conditions.

I wanted to hear "I love you more than anyone," so that I could feel special enough to offset the blinding fear of being rejected. I wanted to hear "I will do anything for you," so that I could lean on someone stronger than me. So that they could help absorb my pain. And I believed that this sacrificial servitude was love. But I was wrong.

What I now know: Love just is.

I have learned that love is gratitude. Love is giving. Love is radical self-compassion. Love is creating your own joy. Love is faith. Love is creativity. Love is music. Love is deep breaths. Love is forgiveness. Love is choosing not to to beat yourself or anyone else up. It's a release of tensions.

To practice this, I had to start telling some radical truths about my belief system. Even harder, I began this practice when I felt the most disconnected from love. Heartbroken and unlovable. Alone. Broken. Suffering. Disconnected from myself. Believing the painful thoughts. Desperate to feel love. The suffering forced me to face what I had been avoiding. It forced me to tell myself the truth. Vulnerable. Naked. Embarrassing. And one by one, painful thought by painful thought, I questioned and dug in, and really challenged myself to get to the heart of my beliefs and what was painful about them. And I blew some of them wide open. And I chose new beliefs to practice. And I continue to struggle with some of them. And I continue to practice them.

Sometimes love is so clear, and sometimes I struggle with what love is and looks like and feels like. I get caught up in not knowing if I am acting from love or from fear. If I am telling myself the truth or if fear is talking. My heart often feels heavy and tangled. I think love is a lifelong journey. I learn more each day. And I know so much more than when I started.

But, the most profound and freeing truth I discovered, and now mindfully and consciously work at practicing every day is: I am. Love is.

I can release the notion of lovability because it doesn't exist. Good enough doesn't exist, worthiness doesn't exist. I am. I don't have to be enough. I am. I don't have to be worthy. Love isn't contingent upon others deeming you worthy of it. Happiness, joy, aren't contingent upon enough-ness, worthiness. They just are. Accessible when we connect to love. When we don't separate ourselves from it. And the only thing that really separates us from love is fear. And the more we practice mindfulness, the more we can consciously choose to connect to love.

I felt unloved and unlovable and I suffered and suffered until one day I decided not to. And it clicked. Love is a practice. Love is completely unconditional. And I have decided to practice love.

Michelle Reinhardt

I had no idea what self love was. I had never given it much (if any) thought. I thought self love was self-centered. If I put myself first, I was selfish and conceited. Loving myself was prideful and made me self absorbed. Owning my gifts, or even considering that I had unique gifts and talents to share, was egotistical and boastful.

Nothing could be further from the truth.

I used ignoring, chastising, despising and shaming as forms of motivation. I believed that self loathing and mean girl tactics were the way to get things done. Clearly my way was not working.

Loving and believing in myself is the key to unlocking the prison called 'not enough.' Being locked in my self-created prison kept me hidden and scared, insecure and trapped in an existence of pain, fear, doubt and dependency. I looked to others to do the loving for me. You love me so I can love myself. You 'tell' me through your approval when I deserve to feel okay and then I will. I morphed into who I thought people wanted me to be and lost my sense of self, desires and dreams.

In one of our Rowdy calls, Meadow said, "We don't create love. We are love." Those three simple words struck a cord deep within. Straight to the heart and beyond the incessant chatter. A felt sense. A wake up call. The truth.

I instantly wanted to figure out the "how" part of it. How do we love ourselves? How do I do this right? Yet there is nothing to figure out. It is just the way. The lack of love is the rejecting of self. I love because I am love. Rejecting that love is just fear and ego and it feels bad because it isn't truth.

It's been a challenge to learn how to love myself. I have a plethora of perceived inadequacies and the voices proclaiming 'failure, goofball, inadequate, weak, pitiful, and lazy' are strong, familiar and loud. A coach asked if I would speak to a child the way I speak to myself. I thought of my six year old daughter. Visions of her ebullient and playful spirit, dancing eyes and joyful belly laughs, huge presence and joie de vivre flashed through my mind. It crushed me to think of my daughters believing that they were anything less than brilliant. It also dawned on me that I deserved nothing less either.

I heard someone say we are worthy of love because we are here, because we were born, because we are breathing. A deep knowing of this truth rose up from my heart. This knowing is another gift of trusting, loving and believing in the beauty of me. I notice it more as I allow the love in and use it as a compass to guide me.

Here's what I know. I can't hate myself thin. I can't despise myself rich and I can't berate myself into love. The answers lie in the softness, the compassion, the appreciation and forgiveness. Through the gentleness and quiet I can hear my Soul. I connect with myself and the Divine. Through the kindness and love I am able to give freely and be generously loving, compassionate and present. Self love has opened up a whole new way of living and being and I am grateful for how it's allowed me to show up in the world in a more authentic and real way.

ROWDY UP

We always have the option to choose love. Often we don't make this choice because we think that by choosing love, we let others 'off the hook.' Or we tell ourselves that they don't 'deserve' our love. We think that by closing and hardening our hearts, we punish the people around us. Or that we are protecting ourselves from pain. And we are wrong. The only one punished by a closed heart is ourselves. And the only thing we protect ourselves from is from the privilege of allowing ourselves to experience love. Choosing love is a practice of self-kindness.

Things I love.

_____

Places I love.

_____

People I love.

_____

Animals I love.

_____

Jobs I love.

_____

Products I love.

_____

Books I love.

_____

Songs I love.

_____

Poems I love.

_____

Movies I love.

_____

Holidays I love.

Food I love.

Drinks I love.

Activities I love.

Quotes I love.

Chapter 14
. . . .

A Rowdy is willing to delay instant gratification to create long term well-being.

Kathie Marshall

I abhor waiting. I like instant. I have walked out on more doctor appointments than I can count. I believe leaving people just sitting around in germ-infested waiting rooms with nothing but old magazines and early 90's décor to amuse us is how serial killers are made.

I think email is too slow and a bad internet connection is the work of the devil. I eat all my meals out of the house (what's that room with all those appliances?) and the week I went without a cell phone was my own personal journey through hell.

I literally have zero patience and I will 100% leave without you if you take too long to get to the car. This goes for my husband and my two year old. Hey, don't judge me. She could walk faster if she really tried.

So how ironic is it that I am writing about the Rowdyism of delaying instant gratification for long-term well-being? Don't bother answering. You already took too long and I have moved on.

I like instant gratification because I like feeling good now. I dislike long-term because it requires me to wait for the prize.

There is no area of my life where instant gratification vs. long-term health has shown up more than diet and exercise.

I have a secret shame to share with you, dear reader. Get your judging face ready. I haven't exercised in three years.

That's not the worst part. Wait for it. I also own a Pilates fitness company. So fitness is basically my whole life.

I knew you would judge. But hear me out, I completely would have if they would just invent a workout I can do only one time and lose five to ten pounds. Come on, that is really not asking too much. After all, we have been to outer space, people, and that seems *much* harder.

So in three years I haven't exercised or stopped myself from eating one thing I have felt like eating. I've completely lived my life according to the whims of instant gratification.

And believe it or not, I haven't lost any weight, gained any muscle and I still can't run a 5k.

And here I am, three years older.

A little saggier. A little lumpier.

And I started to try and find the culprit. Universe? God? Society? Who is going to man up and take responsibility for this?

Sigh. I guess I better raise my hand. It took me a good long while but I finally realized the one flaw with instant gratification: when you only choose short-term the effect is still long-term. It's never accomplishing any goal other than satisfying the immediate urge of the moment.

I repeatedly trade Kathie-in-six-months' happiness and success for Kathie-right now. For cake now. Or for TV now. For less effort right now. But Kathie-right-now doesn't pay the high price. Kathie-in-the-future does.

So why care?

Because six months comes freaking quickly. So does five years. So does ten years. And honey, I am sorry to say but them thighs ain't getting any fitter just thinking about exercise.

My impatience for results *right now* has generated zero results. And I think I've finally learned that long-term is as instantly gratifying as you can get. My brain can accept this. My brain wants to make sure we are operating on the quickest path possible and when your end goal is a fit healthy body - the shortest route there is long-term. Multiple workouts in multiple months with very slow changes – that is as short-term as is possible in this situation. Brain and body shake hands.

Lately though even Kathie-right-now is liking this long-term thingy. The sexy of long-term lies in the feelings you get to feel right now while pursuing your long term goal.

Like pride, or kindness, or accomplishment. And those feelings are my new instant gratification.

These are all emotions I get to feel every time I choose to follow through for long-term-Kathie. And I like feeling these things. I like making these choices. And I'm pretty sure that Kathie-in-six-months will like these choices too.

ROWDY UP

To create lasting change our desire to reach our goal has to be stronger than our weakness for instant gratification. The long-term has to have precedence and veto power over the short-term. This is about the long-haul. Our target. Our mission. If we don't want it enough. We won't get it. Period.

What do you want?

_____

What do you really really want?

_____

What will you have to delay in order to get what you really want?

_____

What discomfort are you willing to accept in order to achieve your long-term desire?

_____

What will you have to believe to make delaying the instant gratification tolerable?

_____

What do you need to remember when you're reaching for that instant 'hit' of gratification?

_____

What will make you proud of yourself?

_____

Why do you know you can do it?

_____

What promise are you willing to make?

_____

Are you willing to keep your promise? Why or why not?

_____

Chapter 15
. . . .

A Rowdy grows herself up.

Audrey Wilson

"I'm a little jealous of Em. Some days I'd like to just sell everything, pack up what I need, hit the road and go somewhere new."

I wrote those words after I watched my daughter pull out of our driveway to start her trip across the country and begin her new life. Later, as I read what I'd written, I quickly dismissed it as a far off, impossible dream.

At the time, the only thing standing between me then and me now was an immense mountain of doubt. Doubt that I was brave enough to do something that bold, all by myself.

You see, I'd always believed that someone or something outside of myself was the boss of me. They'd tell me what to do - or do it for me if I pouted enough - and then they'd come along to clean up any messes I'd made. Like a Mommy. And like a baby lulled to dreamland in her mother's arms, I was blissfully content to live that way.

In my former world it was a rite of passage to be the clueless country club wife who relinquished all awareness of her financial life. As long as the VISA bill got paid every month and I could remain knee deep in the designer handbags and jewelry, who cared?

After my divorce, armed with a sweet alimony deal, I fiddle-dee-dee'd my way around money and thought, like Scarlet O'Hara, that I'd just worry about that tomorrow. Someone should have better prepared me for how to manage my finances and things like taxes, and home and auto repairs! But since no one did I just figured that if it got really bad, Someone would come along and fix it for me. A prince, the lottery, a fairy godmother; any of those would do.

I was seething on the inside with a smile plastered on my face. People were always betraying or disappointing me, or just not acting the way they should so that I could feel good. Because other people, places, and even sometimes the weather were always out to get me, I sat around really pissed off or sad, albeit in designer clothes and luxury sedans. I abdicated my entire emotional life to things like the line at Starbucks being too long or to other people's moods and behaviors.

Before I found *the Rowdies* I'd already begun the work of unraveling some of my painful beliefs, but nobody invited me to challenge my thinking the way they did.

I was forced to look at the truth of my life, measured not in the stories of victimization and helplessness that I told, but in the results I couldn't deny. I was in debt, overweight, and emotionally immature.

And nobody was coming to save me. I had to become my own hero.

With daily Rowdy work I began to take responsibility for my life, my body, my finances, and my feelings. I made choices and I accepted the consequences.

So when that far off desire to leave behind the life I'd known came knocking, I knew I could do it.

I went on a road trip and found my new home in the Historic District of a southern city, ten miles from the ocean, and I started the work of moving on. I took charge of the repairs and selling of my house, making confident - not fearful - decisions. I embraced uncertainties like, what if my house didn't sell? I trusted myself when people questioned what I was doing. I proved to myself that I could do hard things. I didn't fall apart when buyers backed out. When an inspector said my chimney was crumbling, I didn't. I stood firm with people I had once depended on to tell me how to think and feel.

I grew up.

There were many days I told *the Rowdies* it was too hard and that I just wanted Someone to come and do it for me. But instead of hand-holding or coddling, they told me I was born for this and that they had my back.

The road to growing myself up has been the most rewarding I've ever taken. It meant looking at the truth, head on. Giving up all the stories I used to keep myself helpless and small. Letting go of the fantasy that someone else would save me.

I moved 700 miles and a mountain of doubt, and now I know that I can do anything. I am the boss of this new life of mine, and while I'd spent a lifetime believing I wasn't up for the job, I wouldn't give it up for anything...or Anyone.

As I sit here today in my sun-drenched home that contains only what's meaningful to me, I can feel *the Rowdies* here beside me, and they're not surprised.

I was born for this...and more.

ROWDY UP

Growing yourself up means taking responsibility for yourself and your life. It means becoming your own hero and saving yourself. Physically, emotionally, financially, socially, completely. It means being way stronger than you ever thought possible. And it means creating unlimited freedom by dropping your dependency on others.

What windfall/lucky break/knight-in-shining-armor do you think might make your life easier?

_____

What do you hope that you won't have to do all by yourself?

_____

How are you willing to take complete responsibility for your financial life?

_____

How aren't you willing to take complete responsibility for your financial life?

_____

Who or what do you wish would help you financially?

_____

How are you waiting to be saved financially?

_____

What would it mean - financially - to grow yourself up?

_____

How are you willing to take complete responsibility for your physical health?

_____

How aren't you willing to take complete responsibility for your physical health?

_____

Who or what do you wish would help you physically?

_____

How are you waiting to be saved physically?

_____

What would it mean - to your physical health - to grow yourself up?

_____

How are you willing to take complete responsibility for the state of your relationship (or lack of)?

_____

How aren't you willing to take complete responsibility for the state of your relationship (or lack of)?

_____

Are you waiting for your partner (or potential partner) to save you? If so, how?

_____

How are you waiting for your relationship (or lack of) to be saved?

_____

What would it mean - to the state of your relationship (or lack of) - to grow yourself up?

_____

How are you willing to take complete responsibility for your emotional well being?

_____

How aren't you willing to take complete responsibility for your emotional well being?

_____

Who or what do you wish would help you emotionally?

_____

How are you waiting to be saved emotionally?

_____

What would it mean - emotionally - to grow yourself up?

_____

How are you willing to take complete responsibility for your life?

_____

How aren't you willing to take complete responsibility for your life?

_____

Who or what do you wish would help your life be better?

_____

How are you waiting for your life to be saved?

_____

What would it mean - to your life overall - to grow yourself up?

_____

Chapter 16
. . . .

A Rowdy does courage as a verb.

Kathie Marshall

Yesterday I went to the funeral of a man who died of complications from alcoholism. I sat on the hard wooden bench in the funeral parlor packed with his friends and family and listened to the muffled conversations and quiet tears.

Hearing about this man's last years, months and days, I couldn't help see the parallels between our lives. Choosing to not use drugs didn't always feel like a choice, and when things don't feel like a choice, they feel like a prison. Hell on earth.

Closing my eyes from the dim light streaming in from the mosaic windows I reflected upon my own recovery - and realized what a miracle I am.

The comforting warmth of the room and the lull of the minister's voice drew me back in time to the vivid memories I sometimes pray I could erase.

I remember the look in my parents eyes the day I told them I was an addict.

I remember the day I stole my mom's bank card for drug money.

I remember relapsing and terror.

I remember cutting my arms with a knife to feel anything but what I was feeling inside.

I remember choosing drugs over everything. Anything.

I was trying to come up with an analogy to describe addiction for those who are confused by how seemingly normal people destroy their own existence in the pursuit of a tiny baggie of white powder.

My attempt at explaining the unexplainable is this. Your mind is an apartment where you have lived alone your whole life.

And then you try *your* drug. The one that helps you become everything you have always wanted to be. Powerful, confident, attractive.

And just like that, your mind gets a roommate.

At first the roommate stays out of the way. Only comes out occasionally and in your mind it is still your voice you hear. But as time goes by the roommate's voice gets louder and louder until it starts to drown out your own. Eventually the roommate takes complete control. You are but a whisper of a voice. You have been nearly quieted completely.

I said yes over two thousand times.

Until the night I said *no*.
And this is how I know Rowdies do courage as a verb.

I knew I could come back to my Rowdies, my girls, and tell them I said yes. I could tell them anything and they would be my cheerleaders, my champions.

But when the moment of choice came, I felt them all standing over me. Loving me. Regardless of my decision.

And I said no.

I watched as my past walked towards the bathroom held in the palm of a friend's hand.

I almost followed.
I almost called to her.
But I didn't.

I took a deep breath – and left the party.

There was no parade. No high fives. Nothing to commemorate the decision I had just made. It was just me, left in this world with all its ups and downs, with all its chaos and insanity. And I finally saw that as a gift, not a punishment.

That is the only difference between this man and myself. I decided to lean into this life. He decided to leave it. Neither of us is right or wrong. We both found peace. If you ask any addict, that is our only wish.

ROWDY UP

Courage isn't something we feel. It's something we do. It is the unwillingness to buckle under the weight of fear. It's the belief that love is the highest power. And that by acting from a place of love, and choosing to do courage, we tap into a power greater than anything we can imagine.

What do you want?

_____

What kind of courage will be necessary to create your desired outcome?

_____

What courage does your higher self/soul know?

_____

Do you believe that change is possible?

_____

Are you willing to be uncomfortable?

_____

Are you willing to let the old part of you die to go into the unknown?

_____

What will courage do?

_____

What will happen if you surrender your fear and move forward with love?

_____

Are you willing to forgive yourself immediately?

_____

Are you willing to expect that you will go off track?

_____

Are you committed to re-aligning with your desired destination?

_____

Are you willing to practice self-love and open-heartedness?

_____

What actions are required?

_____

Are you willing to fully commit to the awareness that is necessary?

_____

What will that (commitment to awareness) look like?

_____

Chapter 17
. . . .

A Rowdy sets boundaries and burns manuals.

Meadow DeVor

Listen.

We all have them.

Some of us have long ones. Some of us have short ones. Some of us have nice ones. Some of us have mean ones. Some of us pretend to not have them at all. And some of us just whip 'em out at any old time, and use them as manipulative weapons of mass destruction.

No matter the size, the length or the age.

We always keep these hidden from sight. And we know the entire thing by heart.

On page 42 it might say, "If you see that I'm upset, you're supposed to ask me what's wrong."

On page 128 it might say, "If it's Christmas, you're supposed to know what I want and get it for me."

On page 387 it might say, "When you see a beautiful woman, you're supposed to be struck blind momentarily and give me extra attention just because she walked by."

On page 956 it might say, "When you're upset, you're supposed to talk to me and make me feel included."

Basically, we carry around encyclopedia-set-sized invisible instruction manuals titled "How You Should Make Me Happy; Volumes I - Infinity."

The problem is that these manuals are an ongoing project. There are indefinable loopholes. And horribly irrational penalties. There are blatant contradictions everywhere. Constant edits and ceaseless reprints. Written and re-written to offer an endless supply of hoops for the people in our lives to jump through.

And our people?

They always fail.

Because no matter how much we love someone.

No matter how kind we are.

How smart we are.

How cunning we are.

It's impossible to follow all of the rules. All of the time.

Because it's impossible to be in charge of making someone else happy.

Joy. Happiness. Peace. Love. Gratitude.

These are not states of being that can be created for another human being.

We've been seriously duped into thinking that someone else can make us feel something. We've been taught to believe: You followed my rule = I am happy. You didn't follow my rule = I am mad/sad/jealous.

But here's the truth: Happiness can't be given to you by anything other than you.

We are happy when we choose to believe happy things. When we choose to focus on the positive. When we choose to love.

And this has nothing to do with whether or not someone followed your rule.

People break rules. They screw up. They check out a girl's ass. Or forget your birthday. They text too much. Or not enough. They ignore you when you're sad. Or forget to pick up toilet paper at the store.

And if we've set ourselves up to make our emotional state dependent on another person's ability to follow our invisible manuals.

Then we lose. Every time.

And what about boundaries? Right? That's what every student asks after they learn that they've gotta burn their manuals. They mistakenly believed that their manuals *were* boundaries. They think that by burning their manuals - they will become doormats of epic proportions. And that's not the case. We've just been really confused about the difference between manuals and boundaries.

If manuals are titled 'How You Should Make Me Happy,' boundaries would be titled *'How **I** Make Me Happy.'*

Boundaries are invisible manuals written exclusively for ourselves. They aren't instructions for another person. They are only instructions for ourselves. They are never written out of anger. Or resentment. Or manipulation. They are never written to make someone else behave. They are only written with the full acknowledgment that people will do what they do. And we get to feel how we feel. And we get to choose to follow through with our own consequences.

On page 2 it might say, "When I don't get a call back. I will send an email instead."

On page 5 it might say, "If you are drunk, I will not have a charged discussion with you. I will leave and come back later."

On page 6 it might say, "When I don't want to do something, I will tell the truth."

On page 11 it might say, "When I am upset, I will take responsibility to bring myself back to calm."

On page 15 it might say, "If I want something for Christmas, I will ask for it. And if I don't get it as a gift, I will make sure to get it for myself."

On page 19 it might say, "When someone is late, I will still hold to my own time frame."

Boundaries are tough. They require a ton of self-awareness, rationality and emotional maturity. They require vulnerability, willingness to uphold consequences, and often they risk the very thing we're trying to protect: the relationship itself.

They prevent us from becoming doormats. And hold us solely responsible for our inner state of being.

Boundaries are about self love. And love of others. They are about caring for yourself and others. They give us new guidelines for inner peace.

And most of importantly.
They work.

ROWDY UP

Writing out our manual by putting words to paper is a powerful demonstration of the conditions that we put on our own happiness. It helps us identify many of the subtle manipulative techniques that we use in our relationships. Humor and mockery are powerful coaching tools - writing out our manual from this perspective helps us lighten up and laugh at ourselves so that we can change our behavior.

How You Should Make Me Happy; Volumes I - Infinity. The rules and regulations that must be followed in order for me to experience positive feelings:

If _____, you should _____.
When _____, you should _____.

1.

2.

3.

4.

5.

6.

7.

8.

9.

10.

11.

12.

13.

14.

15.

16.

17.

18.

19.

20.

How I Make Me Happy. The rules and regulations that I have for myself to create my own wellbeing.

When _____, I will _____.
If _____, I will _____.

1.

2.

3.

4.

5.

6.

7.

8.

9.

10.

11.

12.

13.

14.

15.

16.

17.

18.

19.

20.

Chapter 18
. . . .

A Rowdy does grace not force.

Susan McCusker

Eager to please. Anxious to do it right. The desire to be a star student, and therefore someone special.That has been the recurring theme of my life. And those desires were in full effect, standing there in the barn. The smell of horse and hay strong in my nose.

I was here to learn. I had taken the dive, and finally acted on a life-long desire to learn to ride a horse. Tonight was the first time I would tack up by myself. My trainer, Maria, stood there to watch. The normal flurry of activity started in my heart: do it right the first time, impress Maria, act as if I know more than I really do.

Except I was stuck. I needed to lower the horse's head over my shoulder so that I could get the bit in her mouth, and the bridle secured. But when I reached up and started trying to pull Fluffy's head down she didn't budge. So I put a little more force into it and pulled down harder. She merely tossed her head and looked away from me. I could feel my heart beat a little harder. Why couldn't I do this? Why was I being such an idiot? This could not be that hard. I had seen children do it for goodness sake.

I tried again. Put a little shoulder into it this time. There may have been grunting. Maria watched me and said one word: "Relax." She grabbed my arm and flopped it around: "RELAX, "she said, a little louder than before. I was mortified. Again I tried. Again Fluffy merely snorted and turned her head away. Maria started laughing. Then she said something that changed everything.

"Do you really think you're going to force a 1000 pound horse to do what you want it to do?"

I was dumfounded. Instant awareness that I was not actually going to physically overpower a 1000 pound horse seeped in. My defenses dropped. And for the first time that night I was ready to learn. I was humbled. I took a deep breath and calmed myself. I looked at Fluffy. Clucked softly, and rested the lightest touch possible on her neck. She immediately lowered her head over my shoulder. Nuzzled me for a moment, and then dipped down to be bridled.

As we walked to the arena, my brain was going crazy, realizing all the implications this had for my life. It was like the pieces of a puzzle were falling into place. A mantra started in my mind:

Force does not equal control.
Force does not equal control.
Force does not equal control.

Force can be an interesting word. It has a lot of negative connotations. But at heart, I think it's the belief system that if you just push harder, or longer, or further, you will get what you want. It's the belief that things have to be hard, or even that suffering is required. Force is difficult. Challenging.

Draining.

The aftershocks of this enlightenment have not been small. I have seen a hundred situations in my life where I use force in order to control: with my dogs, with my children, with my husband, and most of all, with myself. But force is not love. And force is definitely not grace. Dropping my forceful nature has not been easy. In a sense, at times, it feels like giving in. Surrendering. Letting go. Sometimes I feel a little lost in space without it. I had believed that force grounded me. It made feel that I was actually in control of lots of things. Without force, what was there?

Which brings us to grace. Oh how I love that word. I have aspired to grace for most of my life. Yet ironically, I have always believed that it would be force that would get me there. I see the humor in this now; Grace and Force are diametrically opposed. I can use force for the rest of my life and never get to grace. Because Grace is not a destination. It is a state of being. You cannot arrive at Grace. You cannot map a journey out toward Grace. Rather, one thought at a time, one moment at a time, one incident at a time, you can CHOOSE grace.

A soft cluck.

A gentle hand.

A nuzzle.

That's where grace is found.

Tina Sederholm

'If you want to look at the view, stand still. Otherwise watch where you put your feet.'

So said our guide before we set off. We were a group of modern day pilgrims, splashed out in red and yellow waterproofs, about to walk across the Burren, an area of pre-historic limestone pavements, patterned with deep fissures called 'grikes' and slabs of limestone called 'clints'.

I trusted our guide. He had the wind-blasted complexion and the roughened, swollen hands of a man who knew the territory. Mindful that I can be clumsy, prone to tripping over and twisting my ankles, I knew I would be easy prey for the shifting landscape, so for once I let go of my ingrained desire to be first past the post.

And people did stumble and fall. Sometimes a foot would get stuck at an untidy angle, and its owner would have to nudge and wiggle it until it released. Other times a fellow walker would reach out suddenly as their companion pitched towards them. Not me, though. Instead, the advice that I had given out to many of my riding students floated into my mind.

"Let your joints absorb the movement of the horse like the suspension of a car absorbs the bumps in the road."

Perhaps the ultimate humility; taking the advice I had doled out to so many over the years. But I let my hips soften and my knees flex and to my surprise, the girl who was always tripping over in her hurry to get to her next destination was as surefooted as the goats grazing on the harsh land.

Naturally, our final destination was a pub. Supping on Guinness and whiskey, and breathing in the sweet fug of a peat log fire, we swapped stories of our day. A fiddle player struck up a tune, joined by another drumming a tipper against a bodhran. A fellow traveller, a man I rather liked, tilted his head and raised an eyebrow. Of course I wanted to dance. But I dance by myself, in a whirling dervish kind of way. Even in ballroom dancing lessons, I never got the hang of dancing with someone else. I would stiffen up, get ahead of the music, and bump into my partner in my efforts to anticipate the next move. Still, I nodded yes, and sent out a quick prayer that his hiking boots were equipped with steel toecaps.

But I had changed that day on the Burren. With no fierce grasping for the end destination, I was in a state to listen and follow. Not in a subservient way, but in a flow back and forth. I knew exactly what to do. I let my hips soften and my knees flex, and I danced in perfect time with him.

I have had to repeat this lessons many times. I still get seduced by the idea if I try harder, push stronger, I will get everything done....but it never works. Usually I fall over. Like yesterday, slipping on ice as I hurried towards the next lesson I was due to give. And as I got up, brushing the slush from my backside and contemplating the bruise that would flower there later, I remembered there is another choice. I can let my hips soften and my knees flex...

ROWDY UP

We use force when we try to push or pull something into behaving the way we want. When we try to exert physical power, mental power or strength over reality. When we resist. When we go against the natural flow. When we create unnecessary difficulty and suffering. We try to conquer our challenges. We fight and argue. Instead, we can choose grace. We can choose to move or act with elegance and beauty. We can accept and love. We can refine our movement, our power, our mental acuity and gracefully flow with the natural way of nature and reality. To do grace means to live life in perfect harmony with the way things are.

Pick an area of your life that you tend to try to use force instead of grace.

What would dropping the struggle here look like?

_____

Where am I fighting reality?

_____

Where am I wanting to change the behavior of someone else or the universe?

_____

What would trusting myself look like here?

_____

What payoff do I think I'm going to earn by forcing and struggling?

_____

Is suffering necessary here? Why or why not?

_____

What payoff will I earn by choosing grace instead?

_____

What would choosing grace look like?

_____

What would love do?

Chapter 19
. . . .

A Rowdy knows that life isn't supposed to be fair.

Meadow DeVor and The Rowdies

This isn't fair.

We've all fallen prey to this sneaky little thought. Maybe we're just too run down. Or maybe we've had some unjustified circumstances thrown our way. Or maybe we think that for all the suffering and hard work we've endured - we deserve a goddamned parade.

We look around and other people seem to have it so much easier. Lisa didn't have to work this hard - she's just naturally thin. Jessica's parents put her through college - she didn't have to pay off this debt. Julie's baby sleeps through the night - that's why she's always so nice. Marcy's husband helps her so much - that's why they still have great sex.

We've all been there. Wanting help. Wishing life was different. Easier.

Wishing life was fair.

But wishing for fairness is really painful. Very common. And so toxic. And the truth is: Life isn't fair. And it's not supposed to be.

We exhaust ourselves trying to prove how it should be fair, how it could be fair, how to make it more fair. We try to make our marriages more fair. Our time more fair. Our love more fair. Our kids more fair. Our finances more fair. Our work more fair. Our sex lives more fair.

And it doesn't work.
And it never will.

Life isn't fair.
And it shouldn't be fair.

Indonesia gets hit with a tsunami. We don't. That's not fair.

Twenty little kids go to school and die. Ours don't. That's not fair.

You might struggle with your weight. Other people struggle because they have no food. That's not fair.

There truly is not one single thing in this life that IS fair. That's reality.

But, if we can let life be what it is. Let it not be fair. And stop trying to make it fit our imaginary math equation.

We will find that life isn't fair. And that this is a beautiful thing.

We can point our finger and blame injustice. Or we can raise our hands to the sky in absolute gratitude. It's our choice. And it depends on where we put our focus.

In Rowdyville - I posed this challenge:

Tell me 20 reasons why you are thankful that life isn't fair.

And *the Rowdies* answered. One by one. And their lists were poignant. Inspired. And life changing. Not only for them. But for the thousands of readers that got to read them through my blog.

I urge you to read through these and to take the time to do this for yourself.

Meadow

1. I was born to people who valued questioning authority.

2. I was taught to play music from the time I was able to walk.

3. I had a grandma who adored me.

4. I did not die when I was playing in water and the power line had fallen into it.

5. Getting good grades was ridiculously easy for me.

6. I've always been pretty. (Even when I didn't know I was.)

7. I was able to have a child.

8. I was able to sell my music conservatory and move to the Central Coast.

9. I am able to work a job that I love and support myself and my daughter.

10. I have yoga in my life.

11. I have an iPhone.

12.   I get to start every morning and end every night reading amazing insights from people around the world.

13.   I know how to coach myself.

14.   I was able to be a guest on Oprah.

15.   I have an amazing team of people supporting me 24/7.

16.   I had the courage to leave. And start over.

17.   I had the great fortune to lose all my money and to find my way back.

18.   I had the great fortune of being raised with violence and dysfunction so that I can help others heal.

19.   I know what the truth means.

20.   I believe in love.

Rowdy 1

1. I was born to parents who loved and adored me.

2. I was born to parents who believe in the value of education.

3. I was born to parents who were financially able to provide for me.

4. I married the man I love and my parents love and support him as well as me.

5. I have two healthy and beautiful children.

6. I have lived in two extremely dangerous countries for long periods of time and left unscathed.

7. I bought a house we could not normally afford because the builder was in foreclosure.

8. I can afford to take classes like this one, go to the gym, go to yoga, and have a massage every once in a while.

9. Because my husband is the primary earner, I can choose where/when/how I want to work.

10. I have been able to travel and expose myself to

lots of different countries and cultures.

11. I became a US citizen 10 years ago. And I think there is no better place to be.

12. I have friends I can call upon whenever I need them.

13. My kids love and adore me.

14. We took a chance on a risky overseas assignment that no one else wanted, and had the best experience of our lives.

15. My mom did not die of cancer when I was 4 years old.

16. My daughter survived MRSA when she was 18 months old and living in a third world country. Twice.

17. I was in two earthquakes on the top floor of a poorly constructed 15 floor apartment building.

18. For no good reason, other than Grace, my faith was given back to me after thirty years of missing it.

19. In a dangerous situation, I watched my husband walk out our apartment door and knew that he would lay down his life for me and our children.

20. When I hated and despised my high-paying corporate job, I was able to quit and start work as a catholic school teacher.

Rowdy 2

1.   I've driven drunk and made it home okay.

2.   I had a mammogram and it came back clear.

3.   I was born in the US.

4.   My child was born healthy.

5.   I was able to conceive.

6.   I was able to pay my bills this month.

7.   I drove to work yesterday and made it safe.

8.   The tsunami warning was a false alarm.

9.   We had an earthquake a few years ago and my home and business were unaffected.

10. My mom and sister have had breast cancer and they're still alive and cancer free.

11. I have health insurance.

12. My small business is successful.

13. When I was 17 and hiking in a bad spot, the ground did not crumble when I needed it to stay solid.

14. When that bottle of beer fell off our 12th floor bal-

cony at the hotel it didn't hit anyone.

15.   I found *the Rowdies*.

16.   My dog didn't get hit by that car when the gate was left open.

17.   When our boat ran out of gas in the middle of the ocean, it was only a moment before someone saw us and was able to help.

18.   I pulled my hand back in time to avoid a serious injury.

19.   My plane didn't crash.

20.   I can always call my mom.

Rowdy 3

1. My mother decided to have and keep me although she was only 16.

2. My dad married his pregnant High School sweetheart and last October we celebrated their 40-year love story.

3. At three, I survived a sexual attack and the subsequent hospitalization, both great reminders of my own determination.

4. Met my best friend 33 years ago in 3rd grade, we just had lunch together last Sunday.

5. I have the best childhood memories on my grandparents farm with my cousins.

6. My grandpa was my hero. It was my privilege to hold his hand as he prepared to leave this world.

7. I have the three greatest brothers.

8. My family is dysfunctional. I know this, it has made me a better person.

9. I was fortunate to marry a man who reflected back to me all my fears and how little I thought

of myself.

10. Together we had two beautiful children, the Sun and the Moon in my Universe.

11. I located my strength, fought my way out and started my life for the first time at thirty-five.

12. My parents and two brothers have been very supportive and helpful. The third...well I love him anyway.

13. By the grace of God, I was able to purchase a modest house, in need of a lot of work, but close to my children's school, for my children and I to live.

14. I worked on this house, while I worked on me. Both are more me now.

15. I have a great sister-friend, who helps me remember who I am, when I forget.

16. I have grown from the strength, vulnerability and honesty of *the Rowdies* and our fearless leader, Meadow.

17. I can run.

18. I can dance in my very own kitchen!

19. I have music in my life.

20. I can question my thoughts and laugh at life.

Rowdy 4

1. I was born to a 14 year old in a really small town who was brave enough to give me up for adoption.

2. I was adopted by fantastic parents.

3. I've had the opportunity to travel all over the world.

4. I'm able to say that my favorite pizza joint is in Peru.

5. I grew up going to top private schools.

6. I've never had to look for jobs- they always came to me somehow.

7. I went to college and grad school and never had to take out a loan.

8. My hubby was on my first list of "matches" on e-harmony.

9. I was incredibly reckless in high school and college and didn't die - no joke. I'm still amazed.

10. My big sister is a millionaire and never hesitates

to help me.

11.   I have an amazing network of friends and family that support me.

12.   I've had MS for 11 years and you wouldn't know by looking at me.

13.   My first corporate job paid me a ridiculous salary.

14.   I've found a career that I love at a relatively early age.

15.   Going to college was never even a question for me.

16.   I was able to re-apply and finish my master's degree without having to retake the GRE or fully fill out the forms.

17.   I had an amazing boss who supported me fully when I told him I was leaving his company. He even let me go part time while I finished school.

18.   My hubby and I just took an all expenses paid trip to the Caribbean.

19.   I've had a car since I was 16.

20.   My hubby is completely supportive of me opening my own biz and doesn't get mad when I have a dry spell. Rowdies!

Rowdy 5

1. I had a mom with an endless curiosity and love of learning.

2. My angry, distant, alcoholic father never laid a hand on me.

3. I grew up in safe, beautiful place where I could explore outdoors.

4. I had the freedom to learn things the hard way.

5. I survived some dangerous situations with some very bad people.

6. One day I stopped and never looked back.

7. I got into a great college, paid my way, and graduated debt free.

8. I made it to my mom's bedside in time to hold her hand for her final breath.

9. I was working the day my future husband stopped by the farm.

10. Thirty years later - I love him more than ever.

11. We left security to move across the country and it worked out great.

12. When we came back we ended up exactly where we needed to be.

13. I found my psychologist and I didn't give up.

14. I can work my own schedule and be the parent I want to be.

15. My children are healthy.

16. My inlaws are loving.

17. I have two true, deep, wonderful relationships with girlfriends and a kick-ass big sister.

18. I love my work and I feel proud of my success.

19. I am healthy.

20. I can afford to keep learning and be part of Rowdies.

ROWDY UP

Life isn't fair. And it's not supposed to be. By accepting this, we allow ourselves the freedom to own the beautiful unfairnesses that have been handed to us. Instead of being jealous, we allow ourselves to celebrate one another's wins and triumphs. We choose to have a deep compassion for ourselves and for others rather than struggling to justify and blame. Thank goodness, life isn't fair.

The twenty reasons that I am so grateful that life isn't fair.

1.

2.

3.

4.

5.

6.

7.

8.

9.

10.

11.

12.

13.

14.

15.

16.

17.

18.

19.

20.

Chapter 20
. . . .

A Rowdy believes that she is exactly where she is supposed to be.

Jen Greer

My dad left for Viet Nam when I was a little younger than two. Came home and went back, came home and had a sales job that often took him away for days at a time. He was doing his duty. I thought I'd been abandoned.

I remember my sister being born when I was four and a half years old and it felt like I was abandoned again. Remember starting Kindergarten so scared, one leg sticking up higher than the other when I sat in what we used to call 'Indian Style.' Me, about a foot taller than everyone else. Already seeing clearly how something was wrong with me.

My life's work became trying to fix myself. Swimming fast and getting good grades took center stage. But no matter how hard I tried or how fast I swam or how many A's I earned, I never succeeded.

Most painful part was the anxiety I felt around people. I didn't know what it was back then, just knew that I was perpetually afraid that I'd do that thing that would make them leave. I remember good times too—having fun at swim meets, singing "We Are The Champions" on 12 hour bus rides to Nashville, eating Spring Water Chocolate Chip cookies and playing Frogger at summer club. But there was always this nagging whisper reminding me that at any time I was only one word, action, look, step, etc. away from everything falling apart.

I repeated this pattern in high school, throughout college, into my 20's and 30's. Added binge eating and drinking though. It helped to drown out the whisper and unleash my aliveness— until the next day, when the whisper became a scream and I donned the black cloak of shame.

Now I'm 43 and I've done 10+years of growth work, life has changed. I am less anxious. Much less co-dependent. I've learned about things I love and become part of communities I cherish. This story of rejection is not gone, but it's fading, as is the isolation and lack of love that come with it.

But I think I still tell myself that there is a fairytale, a ghost ship, that should have been mine. The life that should have happened, but didn't. And if only it had happened, I would have five beautiful kids and a jovial husband who adores me and a career that enables me to share my gifts and earn a generous income.

I would have appreciated my youth and beauty when I had it, worn form fitting clothes that showed off my six-foot long-legged athletic frame and danced and laughed and laughed and danced. I'd have so many friends--we would have been in one another's weddings and would be swapping stories of motherhood as we raise our kids. There would be so much love.

If only I had understood sooner what was happening inside me. Sought the right help. Or if only it had never happened in the first place, though that doesn't feel as compelling.

I'm a Rowdy and a committed lover of growth work, so I *know* that when I argue with reality I always lose, but only 100% of the time (to misquote Byron Katie). So why hang onto this belief that it should have, could have been different?

Maybe because releasing the ghost ship means accepting this life as it is—and me as I am. Accepting would mean that it's okay that I'm 43 and haven't been able to conceive a baby. It's even okay if this is due to trauma I hold in my body, trauma I haven't been able to fully release even though I'm a mind body coach. It's okay that I can't truly know the source of my infertility.

It's okay that after 10 years of growth work I'm still wearing training wheels when it comes to letting love in. That while I share my life with many amazing people, it's challenging for me to cultivate easy friendships. It's okay that my husband is having a mid-life crisis of sorts and isn't sure he wants to be married to me. It's okay that I'm not earning much income and feel a bit lost when it comes to work and money. That it's been a few weeks and I haven't been able to choose from between two nearly identical tiles for our kitchen backsplash.

When I give up the fairytale, the story that anything could've been or should've been different; I'm left with what is. I see that I'm just like every other person on this planet, living their lives to the best of their abilities. Some learned to love early and lost. For some money comes easily and love doesn't come at all. Some struggle with weight, some with intimacy, some with alcohol, some with drugs, some with sex.

There are no fairytales. We've all been dealt a hand, each hand uniquely our own. We can complain to God for decades on end that we should have had a different hand, we can stare at it and try to will it into something different, or we can say this is the hand I have, what do I want to do with it?

What do I want to do with my hand of infertility, career and marriage confusion, a mending heart and reluctance to trust?

For starters, see that there's a lot more in my hand. There are people I love. Family members who are alive and with whom my relationships grow more authentic and loving all the time. A sister whom I love more every day. Rowdies for certain.

There is my mending heart, which is more capable of loving with every day. There is a man in my life and in my home - whom I love and am learning to love better all the time, even if our path together is unclear. I am not a super-fit 20-something competitive athlete, and I do have a strong healthy body that I am getting to know better all the time. I have the resources to explore adopting a child, and am slowly learning to put more trust into God and what she has in store for me.

Letting go of the life that wasn't lets me step more fully into the life I have. I leave the fantasy for the reality. The fairytale may look pretty, but it isn't real. This life I have is.

I'm not going to lie. There's grief in letting go of the fairytale and I haven't fully let go yet. And there's a shift in perception that needs to happen to see the whole of this real life as a gift, not just the bright shiny parts.

It feels a little daunting. But already considerably less so than it did a week ago when I first wrote this. And I trust that with the support of *the Rowdies* and the others I love, the Universe and all that I've carried with me, I can step into the real life that is here, waiting for me.

Emily Andrysick

I studied Theater. The good, the bad, and the melodramatic, from Sondheim to Stanislavski. I was *going* to go to New York. To find a big break. To land a big part. To work my butt off, pounding pavement and slinging coffee until I got discovered.

But I had to graduate first. When I was a sophomore in college I decided to transfer schools. It would be easy: I would apply to my dream school, be accepted, and continue as a junior in the fall. Easy as pie. It should all work out.

Except for the University of Virginia's decision: rejected.

So my plan to finish my theater degree and become instantly discovered was temporarily sidetracked. In its place, a year off from school. A temporary gig in Portland, Oregon, nannying and interning at a non-profit. A placeholder until I could get back on the *right* track, towards the *right* dream. The one that was so inconveniently interrupted so my real life could happen.

Portland had other plans. I arrived to find a city that was... brimming. With life and liveliness and committed, passionate people. With exciting work and dramatic weather and beautifully layered culture. With amazing art and even more amazing artists. With well-behaved dogs, hysterical goofball kids, old couples holding hands, and adorable, scruffy-faced men in plaid. And each person I encountered, it seemed, was more in love with their life than the last.

It rubbed off: I fell completely and head over heels in love. In love with the now and not the six-months-from-now. In love with homesick and growing up and wanderlust and awkward and adventure and new and scary. I woke up eager to find more to fall in love with and went to sleep excited to dream about it.

I fell in love with real life. It was exhilarating, and enlightening. And when I left Portland I knew I wanted more.

I went to Manhattan. Having just learned to full-on love the full scope of my life, I was starving for more of it. *More life, more life, more life.* And in Manhattan! The perfect place for a wide-eyed 19-year-old life-junkie.

It was June and I was on the eve of my graduation from a women's program I'd been participating in. I was surrounded by swarms of life-loving soul-sisters. And there was a whole Manhattan full of life all around me. I was untouchable.

But my best friend wasn't. The previous night, she'd been killed in a car accident. I heard from another friend over the phone, in the back of a cab, on my way to a party. I was in Manhattan, drinking life with a fat straw, and she was upstate at the end of hers.

I broke in two.

Everything was wrong. It was wrong that a 19-year-old good, healthy, decent girl had died. It was wrong that my graduation never happened and the reason why was wronger still. It was wrong that I was a subway ride from Broadway, and all I was doing was hiding, crying in my apartment, trying to convince my sweet roommates *no, really, I'm fine, it's just hard is all.*

In the big dream, New York had been a stage, waiting for me to showcase everything I could do. In real life, I wished the city would turn me invisible. Swallow me whole. Put a wall between me and everyone else that was so tall and so thick, nobody would hear me sob and ask - over and over - why things were happening this way.

Until the day I pried myself from my apartment for an errand and some oxygen. And, with the pang of some remembered inside joke or late-night giggle-fest, I lost it. Heaving, snotting, on-my-knees sobs, on a sidewalk in the busiest city in America, in broad daylight. The wall I dreamed up between me and the masses of New York crumbled. I was terrified, but powerless to stop the grief that spilled from me faster than I could breathe.

Nobody stopped. Nobody approached. Nobody glanced. Nothing happened. In a swarm of mid-day, mid-town foot soldiers, I was nothing.

And I realized in a perfect, clear second: of all the places on earth to be when the pain comes... I *was* as invisible as I'd wished, an invisible ball of furious sadness, and I had all of Manhattan to bounce around however I needed to. Rendered completely anonymous in a sea of people, I no longer clung to my apartment to feel. I spread out blankets in Central Park - still grieving, but now in the sunshine. I spent an afternoon walking 7th avenue, sobbing behind ultra-chic sunglasses.

Un-approached, unbothered, unnoticed by the thousands around me. I had all the privacy I could ever want, and all the space I needed to feel my way through enormous loss.

I finished school; The University of Virginia accepted me after a second application. I studied theater, loving it, knowing the whole time that I was bound for big, beautiful, messy, *real* life.

In Portland I learned that real life was worth more than a dream. In New York I learned that real life takes space. In Virginia I learned that any place would only be as good for me as I let it be. And as a Rowdy, I know now, that means I am always where I'm meant to be.

ROWDY UP

There is a beautiful poem by Hafiz that says, "This place where you are right now, God circled on a map for you." When we treat our present moment as a sacred place. As a place intended for us. We find beauty, love and infinite wisdom. We stop fighting reality and start searching for meaning. We can not be anywhere but where we are. We can not change our past. We can only live from this moment. By fully embracing it.

Think about the place where you are right now and answer the questions below.

What is the lesson that I need to learn from this place?

_____

Why has my life brought me here?

_____

Why is this place sacred or divine?

_____

What message is being offered for me to listen to?

_____

What am I resisting about this place?

_____

What would happen if I choose to surrender and to really inhabit this place rather than resist this place?

_____

What part of this am I hoping to skip over?

_____

Why did God circle this place right here for me?

_____

What meaning can I bring to this place?

_____

Who do I really want to be right now?

_____

What will happen if I refuse to do this work?

_____

Chapter 21
. . . .

A Rowdy knows the power of prayer.

Meadow DeVor

I live in one of the most beautiful places on earth. A little piece of heaven surrounded by ranches, farms and ocean in the middle of the California coast line.

This morning, I took advantage of an unusually-blank weekday morning and jumped in my car to go to one my favorite running trails about 20 minutes from my house.

Mornings can be utterly gorgeous in this valley. For the short time that California is green, it's almost arrogant with its vibrancy. Showing off for the sky.

But not today.

Nope. Just grey. Subdued.

Rounding the bend into the valley, to the left you can see all the way into wine country. And the hills beyond. To the right, you look up the valley to the ocean. Beyond the ranches.

And today there was a single horse in the middle of the field.

Surrounded by vultures. In an equidistant circle.

There had be at least thirty of them. Sitting there. Ring-around-the-rosie all facing the horse.

My heart sank. Something is wrong.

I got to my trail but couldn't shake the thought of that horse and those vultures.

Should I have done something? Was something really wrong? What do those vultures know? Why were they there? If the horse ran away - would they follow her? Is the horse sick?

And I got to thinking...

*Does this happen to **us?***

***Is** this happening to us?*

When we are sick, or too tired, or too exhausted... do invisible vultures circle us? (Woo-woo, yes I know. But go with me on this one.) Are they just waiting for us to abandon ourselves?

If we give into despair, or hopelessness or depression - does that give them the signal to feed?

I've found that it only takes one step in the direction of choosing to live. One little action. One tiny decision. And the vultures are vaporized.

They crave helplessness. Apathy. Indifference. And call all their friends and relatives for that feast.

They are repelled by vitality. By life force. By saying yes. By doing something.

As I ran the shore cliff - I patted myself on the back. First, for doing something (running) and keeping the invisible vultures away. And secondly, for coming up with such a nifty little blog post (Yay me).

A short-lived celebration.

On my way home, I turned left and leaned forward over the steering wheel to see if I could see the horse. Silently praying that neither the horse nor the vultures were there anymore.

Between the trees, I could see a truck.

Oh good, someone is helping her.

Driving closer, I saw the horse. And two ranch women. Mud boots up to their knees. The horse running panicked arcs around the back of the truck. One woman with her arms out wide - guarding the other woman who was holding a tiny stillborn foal.

The size of a toddler across her arms.

Absolutely overcome with compassion. Love. Sadness. I stopped my car in tears. Watching the women work. Heartbroken, yet grateful for the lesson.

Knowing now what the vultures knew. And what the horsemama knew. And what every woman who has ever lost a baby knows.

And I realized that the horse was keeping vigil. And those vultures had no hope of getting to that baby.

And that maybe. Just maybe.

Someone is also watching over me. And watching over you.

And that the vultures don't have a chance.

Against a love like that.

Michele Brescia

I said a prayer to the stars; every twinkling, shiny, brilliant star I could see.

And, I said a prayer to all those that I could not see. For every beautiful Superstar, hiding in the Universe.

I said a prayer of connection, of joy, of calmness, of being, a prayer for Grace, for belonging and a prayer for those who are longing for everything and anything.

Rowdy prayers of friendship, spoken straight from the heart. For strength and health and tears that cleanse.

I said prayers for adventure, for humor and for fun. I said a prayer to the vulnerable and for those who want to be.

I said a prayer to the elusive parts that are yearning to be heard; calling to them and daring them to come out and sparkle.

Prayers for self-love, for the Rowdy girl inside that just wants to be loved. I said a prayer to that little girl that she might come out and play. That she might see her truth and shine.

I said a prayer of surrender, for direction, for God to show us the way. Prayers for guidance and understanding.

I said a prayer for LOVE. For big, Rowdy, sparkly, shiny, twinkling, blingy, Superstar LOVE.

I said a prayer for me, for you and for all *the Rowdies*.

Twinkling like stars in the great big sky.

ROWDY UP

It has been said that there are only two prayers. One that says: Please. And one that says: Thank you. If God is love, then prayer means speaking directly to love. Speaking directly to the power of love, the energy of love, the wisdom of love. It is a practice with sincere intention. It is a deliberate act of fierce humility. It's an offering to the universe, to our higher selves, to our souls, to loved ones that watch over us, to divine wisdom, to Love, to whatever we believe God to be. The act of prayer helps us to surrender our illusion of control and hands over our issues to a force and a wisdom that is greater than our own. It gives our lives over to unconditional love. Prayer creates miracles. It shifts our thinking and opens our hearts and our minds.

My thoughts on God -

If I were to speak directly to love, I would ask

_____

If I were to speak directly to love, I would thank

_____

If I were to speak directly to love, I would surrender

_____

If I were to speak directly to love, I would allow

_____

If I were to speak directly to love, I would believe

_____

If I were to speak directly to love, I would know

_____

What would it look like for my heart (and/or our hearts) to be softened and opened?

_____

What would it look like to give this over to a power that is greater than me?

_____

Am I willing to trust in the universe/God/love?

_____

What fears do I have?

_____

What would love say about these fears?

_____

An Invitation
· · · · · · · · · · · · · · · · · · · ·

A Rowdy knows that
love creates community
and that communities
change the world.

Martine LaBreche

I'm sitting on a bench overlooking the water surrounding the San Francisco airport. I'm attending a three-day workshop with other solopreneurs. It's a new life for me. I'm on a fifteen minute break. The sun is warm. The wind is gentle. It's a perfect day.

I hear a roar. This sound is so familiar and music to my ears. My gaze is attracted to the sound. Right in front of me, a plane is taking off.

Watching this big metal bird get off the ground usually charges me with excitement, but not today. Instead, I'm filled with sadness. Tears are rolling down my cheeks. They won't stop.

"I don't belong here. I just don't fit in. This is not my gang. My people are up there, at 35,000 feet. I miss them so much. I wish I could be up there with them."

I don't want to go back into the seminar. This group, in the name of performance, is asking me to change. Too fast. Too soon. It doesn't feel right to me. I feel threatened. I freeze. I just want to crawl in and disappear. I feel judged. I feel inadequate.

I used to fly for a living. I was a well respected flight attendant. Appreciated and loved by my clients, my supervisors, my colleagues. I was good at what I did and I loved my job. I loved the constant buzz of people. Always an adventure.

And I adored the people I worked with. All Rowdies at heart. My crew was my family away from home. My airborne community taught me to think on my own. Life threatening events happen fast. We either prevented them or faced them. As a crew member, you need to be both trustworthy and trustful. Lives depended on this.

They taught me how to say "No." A difficult thing for me to learn.

No, you can't smoke.

No, you can't go to the toilet right now.

No, you can't use your cell phone.

They taught me to take responsibility for my choices, to follow my gut feeling, to build my confidence, to set up boundaries, to ask for help, to ask for what I want, to discover what I like and don't like, to trust myself and others, to be open and just curious, to love loneliness, to dine alone in restaurants, and so much more.

Through my community I learned to be more and more me, and to be comfortable with who I am, to accept myself as is, to depend on myself. At retirement, I believed I had lost this. It was hard on me, and on my family.

I missed the connection so much. I was hungry for more. I needed to find a new Life School to feel alive again. A new community to belong to. After quite a few bumpy flights, I finally landed safely home in my amazing Rowdyville.

I recognized right away; this Rowdy community is similar in many ways to my old community. And it offers a mix of unique features; authenticity, honesty, truth, courage, humor, raw emotion, true connection and beautiful camaraderie are ever-present and available on demand. Compassion and collaboration replaces judgement and competition. This would not be possible without the creative leadership of Meadow, our Master Rowdy and her fabulous coaching.

I keep coming back to *the Rowdies* like a drug addict. I feel good here, I'm learning to be more at peace. Some days, when overwhelmed or stressed, instead of ruminating, I go to the forum or listen to class and I amazingly find comfort and direction. I have this weird love/hate relationship about seeking and dealing with the truth. Especially around money. But, I know the truth is powerful and that it works wonders. So I have hope.

I'm starting to see big and small changes in my world; the shopping mall is less attractive, I'm training daily, I'm less reactive, I'm less argumentative. I have less stress. I have less inflammation. My blood test is the best in years, (fifteen to be exact). It's exciting.

I'm so grateful to have found my community of women and to have *the Rowdies* around. As Barbara Sher says, "Isolation is a dream killer." I believe her.

The opposite of isolation is connection. Connection is powerful. It's life transforming. It's the stuff that binds women to women. It's the force that gets us through the tough moments. And inspires us to greater heights. I'm living it. Whatever seemed impossible before, starts to be feasible now.

Are you a Rowdy looking to shine?

You're more than welcome.

Join the club.

JOIN THE ROWDIES

For more information about upcoming Rowdy Classes, *Tao of Rowdy* study groups, Rowdy Events or to join the Rowdy Community, please visit MeadowDeVor.com.

MEET THE ROWDIES

whose inspired contributions
made this book possible.

Emily Andrysick is an interior decorator for the minds of women who are turned off, lights out, de-fused. As founder and creatrix of BombshellCoaching, Emily leads young women to the magical 4-way intersection where pleasure, power, beauty, and boldness meet (and throw a huge party). She lives in Portland, Oregon with her cat, dog, and hunky fella-man, and loves coffee, candles, and saying "thank you." She's tickled to her toes to be a Rowdy, and so grateful to Meadow and her co-Rowdies for the delicious, wholehearted beauty with which they live their lives. BombshellCoaching.com

Kristen Baker lives her life infused with music and believes that every moment offers the opportunity to be filled by your own song. She is committed to helping others tune into their voice, their song. She works ceaselessly each day to connect more deeply and courageously to her own. With love, compassion, integrity, and authenticity. Kristen craves the chance to work with others to dig deeply, relentlessly, to unearth their truths, fears, dreams. She hungers for the opportunity to be a witness to vulnerability and courage. To connect to the fire of the human experience. To learn more visit: YourComingOut. Com.

Michele Brescia lives in a charming New England town with her husband and three daughters. She is a business leader in Corporate America; managing a global multi-million dollar portfolio. In addition to her day job, Michele recently launched her coaching business; focusing on helping women become kick ass money makers. Michele is a Rowdy at heart - seeking opportunities to be present and joyful in her life. She lives her life by the quote from Les Brown – "Shoot for the moon, if you miss you will land amongst the stars" – and has adopted the nickname Superstar amongst her Rowdies. MicheleBrescia.com.

Pat Davenport has been a Life Coach since 2006. Since then she has continued to grow as a person and as a coach. She is a licensed US Coast Guard Captain who loves to sail. "I want to start a wave of truth in this world. I want to help people learn how to tell the truth – about who they are, what they think and what they feel. We hold back our truth because we're afraid of being rejected. In that, we wind up rejecting ourselves." Pat lives in warm, sunny Naples, Florida. Connect with her at PatDavenportCoaching.com.

Kira DeRito owns a retail seafood market in Olympia, Washington where she makes her home with husband Tony, daughter Sailor and two crazy dogs. She serves her local community with a focus on sustainable, nourishing food and offers a weekly email full of fishy information and easy, fun recipes. Find her online at OlympiaSeafood.com.

Bettina Ende-Henningsen lives in the picturesque medieval town of Lüneburg, Germany, which is part of the metropolitan region around Hamburg. A doctor of medicine, she has specialized in the fields of Neurology and Psychiatry. She is a Certified Psychotherapist. She has lived in the US for five years, participating in a neuroscience research project at the University of Madison, WI. She is a co-author of several neurology textbooks. The mother of two teenage daughters, she nowadays is self-employed, working as a medical expert witness. Her special interests are dancing, classical music, and foreign languages.

Jennifer Greer gently guides women into themselves where they find what they've really been searching for all along. You can reach her through her website at JenGreer.com.

Wendy Kaufman is a writer and a teacher. She graduated with a B.F.A. from NYU's Dramatic Writing Program. She has had her plays produced at Soho Repertory Theatre in New York City and the Contemporary Arts Center, New Orleans. She lives in Southern California with her husband Jon and dogs Carrie and Homer.

Martine LaBrèche lives in Montréal, Québec where she helps busy and overwhelmed individuals rebuild their relationships, health and wealth by breaking free from negative patterns and self-talk that leads to stress and anxiety. Martine is passionate about helping people feel good about themselves. She's a Certified Coach and a Positive Psychology Practitioner who's excited to offer innovative wellbeing programs-in French or English- based on the latest science-approach of Positive Psychology, Mindfulness, Neuroscience and Self-Coaching practice. Meet her at DynamixCoaching.com.

Susan Loucks resides in Bloomington, Indiana, a charming college town located in the rolling hills of Southern Indiana. She lives with her husband and two sons. She teaches at Indiana University and she and her husband own a local real estate firm. Susan is a lifelong learner and is always working to improve herself emotionally, physically and spiritually.

Kathie Marshall is a student of life. Learning and exploring her mind, body and soul to face her truths and grow spiritually. She is also a total hot mess that can rarely find her keys and is never far from a giant cup of coffee. Spend more time with her at Kathie-Marshall.com.

Susan McCusker is on a mission to create the perfect life. Failing that, she can be found avidly reading self-help books, teaching classes, and hanging out with her family. A native of South Africa, she considers herself a global citizen and currently resides in Cincinnati, OH. She is a certified coach, and holds a B.A. in Psychology from the University of Notre Dame. You can check her out at SusanMcCusker.com.

Michelle Reinhardt is a Certified Life and Money Coach (aka Mind Manager, Life Stylist, Inspiration Instigator, Confidence Catalyst). Her mission is to help women know their value, rock their body and own their glow so that they love their days, laugh a lot and have the time and energy to create a life they LOVE. She helps her clients to understand that happiness is an inside job, and also teaches them that ease, flow and FUN are a surefire path to get what you want. To learn more about Michelle and sign up for her GLOWfactor Manifesto go to Michelle-Reinhardt.com.

Tina Sederholm is a poet, writer and raconteur. She performs at festivals, pubs, clubs and poetry nights all over the UK. She has taken her one woman show 'Evie and the Perfect Cupcake' to the Edinburgh Fringe Festival twice, and is currently working on her new show 'You Do Not Have To Be Good.' Author of three non-fiction books and a freelance writer for equestrian magazines, she has also been known to give the odd riding lesson. More about her work, books and recordings can be found at TinaSederholm.com or on Twitter, @cupcakeevie.

Ivonne Senn is the first money coach in Germany. Author of the "... aber richtig" handbooks. It's time to stop waiting and start taking action. And she's here to support you. She will help you to understand how you got to the place where you are now – and how to move towards where you want to be. It might make you angry, frightened, insecure. It might make you hopeful, excited, eager for more. It will change the way you think about money forever. Read more about her at IvonneSenn.de.

Tara Rice Simkins was brought to her knees by the journey through the world of pediatric cancer which forged within her a unique understanding of what it means to potentially lose something very meaningful in your life. In the face of such loss, Tara committed to living an extraordinary life. Tara's message is simple: "We can always decide to fall deeper into love with our lives and to summon the courage to press on no matter what." XOXO + Press on, Tara. Tara focuses her attention on the following: Personal Life Coach & Blogger: Tara-Simkins.com, Childhood Cancer Philanthropist: PressOn-Fund.org and Lawyer: HullBarrett.com.

Piyusha Singh was born and raised in India and now lives in upstate New York with her husband, son, two dogs – and any other animals that have adopted her. She is an academic and a certified Life and Weight Loss coach. She is passionate about teaching and learning, and knows first-hand how women lose themselves and their passion as they navigate the waters of academia. She helps women stay connected to themselves and their passions as they work on their education and careers. She has struggled with infertility and helps women find and walk their specific path through infertility. PiyushaSingh.com.

Michele Smith is a wife, mother, friend and Rowdy. She loves spending time with her husband and sons, hiking in the woods with her dog, running, curling up with a great book and spending summer days at the beach. She coaches her sons' cross-country and track teams and is also a running coach at her local CrossFit affiliate. She is currently training for her first half-ironman triathlon.

Audrey Wilson is a certified Life and Weight Loss Coach who helps women reconnect with their femininity and learn how to create a blissfully self-indulgent, pleasure-packed, wildly exhilarating existence. Your desires. Your sensuality. Your power. Your playfulness. Your crazy, courageously sexy confidence. Audrey tried to over-try, over-suffer, over-please, over-martyr and over-deprive her way to happy. To thin. But she failed. Miserably. So she did a 180, ditched guilt, fear, diets, and hoop-jumping and chose hot, throbbing pleasure. You can find her making mischief in the historic seaside town where she lives or at her website AudreyWilsonCoaching.com.

ABOUT THE AUTHOR

Meadow DeVor is a Master Certified Coach, spiritual teacher, yogi and Rowdy who has devoted her practice to helping women live healthier and more meaningful lives. She believes everyone has the power to deepen their experience, to create freedom and live with more joy. She is the founder and leader of the legendary Rowdy community. She has been a guest on The Oprah Winfrey Show and her articles have been featured in Women's Day Magazine. She is known for her take-no-prisoners approach to coaching, her radical authenticity, and most of all... for her giggle. She is committed to doing serious work while making it as fun as possible. She's the author of *Money Love: A Guide to Changing the Way You Think About Money* and writes a popular blog about money, love, life and other stuff.

She lives with her daughter in San Luis Obispo, California.

You can read more of her work at www.MeadowDeVor.com.

MEADOW DEVOR

Printed in Great Britain
by Amazon.co.uk, Ltd.,
Marston Gate.